ARTICLES

2014-2015

✦✦✦

A COLLECTION

BY

PAUL TN CHAPMAN

Articles 2014-2015: A Collection

All Rights Reserved

Copyright © 2016
Paul TN Chapman
ptnc.books@gmail.com

Please note that the dates under each article title are the dates of publication.

2014

Listen to Your Gut
23 January 2014

The song writer/satirist/mathematician Tom Lehrer once commented that people complained that (other) people don't communicate well any more. He said 'if a person can't communicate, the very least he can do is to shut up.'

This is the first in a series of blogs on various aspects of communication. In this blog I want to outline various elements that will be discussed. I'm somewhat naturally analytical, so for me, communication, verbal more so than written, involves intuition as well as observation.

In the course of my professional life in social service, I developed a strong awareness of the elements of communication. At one point, I had learnt American Sign Language, which was a huge asset even after I ran out of hearing impaired people for whom to sign (I changed jobs). Half of sign language involves facial expression and body language. It's practically impossible to tell a deaf person a lie, because while your hands say 'yes', everything else about you says 'no'.

Communication entails much more than just words coming out someone's mouth and going into your ears. On a subconscious level, you also pay attention to: word choice, word order, tone, inflection and emphasis. You are aware of facial expressions, body language, physical orientation (how the body is angled, the distance from speaker to listener, etc). It might surprise you to realize that you also pay attention to how you viscerally respond to a statement, and also to the images that may come to mind.

Let's take these two examples of the same basic statement.

A) Please pass the salt.   **B)** Pass the salt please.

A differs from **B** only in the order of the wording, but **A** conveys a simple request, while **B** suggests an expectation, perhaps a politely worded demand, and also a sense of relationship (which I'll discuss in a moment). Of course, **A** spoken with clenched teeth suggests you might not survive the meal if you don't pass the salt, and **B** with an emphasis on the *please* suggests your fellow diner is in desperate need of sodium chloride, and may even be somewhat exasperated owing to its immediate non-delivery.

Did you know that a person can also communicate his/her sense of relationship as well, even in a few words? Taking example **B** (pass the salt please) the speaker implies that you don't actually have a choice because in your interpersonal relationship, you are considered subordinate to the speaker. I once made changes to the settings on someone's computer (at her request). When her husband discovered this, he said, 'Change it back please,' but there was no question that this was anything but a casual command. His tone was civil and non-threatening, but he wasn't looking at me when he spoke (he was reading his mail); the lack of eye contact and his physical orientation made it clear he had no investment in persuading me, he simply expected it to be done. You don't have to engage someone (as you would by means of eye contact) when you're the superior.

Eye contact is also important because it communicates, among other things, the speaker's investment in his statement. A man once introduced me to a group of people as 'our friend,' but we all noticed that he was staring off into space as he spoke, and something felt wrong to me when he said it. He didn't really believe it. It has since been confirmed that I am on the outermost periphery of this individual's social orbit and affections. Of course, too *much* eye contact can have the opposite effect—'look at me because I don't want you looking anywhere else.'

All these factors that I've described come from the speaker, and are under the speaker's conscious (but not subconscious) control. There are two factors that the speaker does not control, and are very persuasive: your visceral response, and the mental image a statement may conjure.

We respond viscerally (instinctively, as I'm using it here) with different parts of our body. I usually have a gut response. When I was told to 'change it back please,' I felt tightening in my stomach, and distinctly subordinate. I once listened to a *theoretically* charismatic lecturer delivering a short speech. He used a lot of exciting sounding words, tonal inflections and gestures; the audience seemed quite stimulated by what he said. However, as I was leaving, my stomach felt empty and unsatisfied. I realized that although he *sounded* wonderful and learned, the lecturer hadn't actually said a damned thing!

Mental images are important too! Early in my career, I met with a young couple who were having some marital difficulties. As the husband spoke, I had the mental image of him, dressed in an oilskin, piloting a small boat through stormy seas while his wife was battened down under the hatches. When I mentioned this image, his wife said, 'That's *exactly* what it's like!'

Listen to your gut!

✦✦✦

Terms of Persuasion
29 January 2014

Language is one of our most civil means of persuasion; we are exposed to persuasion every day. You will find more alluring 'a sleek, sassy, sexy car' than 'a boxy bubblebug', even though it's the same vehicle. In the 1920's, the Studebaker Corporation made a series of automobiles called the President, the Commander, and the Dictator. Persuasive names created marvellous visions. In-house, the Dictator was Model GE, which wouldn't have sold nearly as well.

When someone hires me as a consultant, I am clear about what I will do; I clarify the purpose of my engagement. I do not talk down to people, or over their heads. I earn their trust and respect; if I make them feel helpless or stupid, I deserve neither their trust nor their respect. I try my best to avoid 'conning' my clients.

During the last year, I attended three or four really top-drawer workshops, given by presenters who excited and informed me. I knew more when I left than I had when I arrived. Each presenter had something to say, said it in plain language, and then stopped talking. My confidence and admiration for these professionals were, and remain, boundless. They clearly knew more than I, and I was comfortable with that—that's why I went!

In the same time frame, I also attended workshops about establishing oneself on the job market, establishing a business, networking, and self-promoting. It's disheartening that so many of these workshops seemed more like classes in 'The Art of the Con'.

Language must evolve; else would we yet speak the speech that spake Shakespeare (or words to that effect). But is it necessary to *invent* terms? Sometimes an expression will evolve from a particular situation, but when taken out of its original context, can develop the *opposite* meaning. The term 'red herring' for example, referred to the training of fox-hunt hounds to stick to the fox's trail and not be distracted. Now it means a false clue.

The very first orientation speech I attended was full of clichés and effete language; I had little confidence in the presenter or her services—she didn't have much to say, but we weren't to know that. On the surface she appeared professional and impressive. On the surface, that is.

A 'rule of the con': the less you have to say, the more you must talk. It prevents people from thinking, or at least, understanding. Therefore, they will need you more.

Many other workshops I attended drowned in 'specialized language'. We were being talked to from On High by Those Who Had Already Succeeded; somehow, we were communicating (if you could call it that) across a vast chasm with a Supreme Intellect. These were meant to be 'peer presentations', but it felt more like the handing down of the Ten Commandments. Moses may have felt this way, but when God said, 'Thou shalt not steal,' there was no ambiguity.

Another presenter talked about networking and informational interviews. He explained that when he'd acquired the information he needed, he sent out 'asks' (not requests for an interview). That was silly and annoying, and it made him seem corny. (The baby's pacifier is now called a 'binky', but no one I know can explain why. Would you not feel foolish asking for a 'binky'?)

Still another presenter spoke of 'value statements', her version of the term 'elevator speech'. Both are an oblique way of saying, 'tell me about yourself and what you want,' which seems to me a better, clearer way of putting it.

In fairness, none of these presenters meant any harm, and probably were unaware of a secondary effect they were having. While they were sounding dazzling and impressive, because they wanted to help, they were also creating a potential for distrust. This is called *Mutual Arising*, and is described in the second verse of the Tao Teh Ching. Loosely translated: *When all see beauty as beauty, ugliness arises.* If you identify a specific group within a population, for example, everyone else becomes 'non-group.' You have two groups, when you only meant to have one. In this instance, 'you may lead me to trust you, or to distrust you.'

There is a reason for this approach. You, the prospective client, need be *persuaded* that these professionals function on a level that's over your head. (Or, to put it another way, the *professional* needs *you* to be persuaded.) If they succeed, you will see them as credible and lofty; you'll be more likely to give them your time/money/attention.

Another 'rule of the con': a confused person is easier to handle. Elitist language can be very confusing. Vague language and an air of superiority are guaranteed to produce a rich level of befuddlement.

When people spout effete language, my confidence in them wavers. Why don't they speak plainly and say what they mean! When I hear cliché after cliché, or language I've never heard before, I wonder what I'm *not* supposed to know. Perhaps Lewis Carroll's King, in *Alice's Adventures in Wonderland* put it best: '*Begin at the beginning,' the King said, very gravely, 'and go on till you come to the end: then stop.'*

The chief virtue that language can have is clearness, and nothing detracts from it so much as the use of unfamiliar words.

Hippocrates

I'm persuaded.

※

How to Write Effectively
3 February 2014

A couple of times over the last eighteen months, people have asked about 'how to write a story', and I've read some samples that were energetic and ambitious, but not quality writing. (I say this fully aware that I am growing as a writer, and am more guilty of failed composition than of good writing.) I say that what I read was not quality writing, not only because of mistakes in grammar, but because certain preparations had not been made.

All creativity begins in your head. Unquestionably the absolutely-must, 100%-required, don't-leave-home-without-it necessity is this: **_Believe in yourself_**. If you aren't thoroughly convinced you can start and complete this writing project, you are doomed from the start.

Certain steps are obvious. You have to know your subject, your purpose in writing, and who you want to reach. You need some plan for telling the story (the outline is helpful).
Other steps *should* be obvious, but in the excitement of 'becoming an author' and the enthusiasm to 'tell the story', often are missed. To accomplish this, you have to have 'tools'.

What are your tools? Read other writers' work and expose yourself to as many different styles, and as many different genres, of writing as you can. Read many different authors within each genre. Read mysteries, if that's your interest, but read poetry and non-fiction as well. Although you are writing a non-fiction article, exposure to fictional writing may help you reach a larger audience because of some literary technique you discover. Reading poetry helps build a rich vocabulary, and a sensitivity to phrasing that can turn a mundane sentence into something truly compelling. The larger your vocabulary, the greater the richness and sensitivity with which you can write. By reading 'outside your area', you collect bits of fact than can be useful in giving your writing substance.

Let's say you want to write fantasy stories. You should read JRR Tolkien, Piers Anthony, Spider Robinson, Lloyd Alexander and others. Include some of the older children's stories like *Mary Poppins* and *Wind in the Willows*. Elements that are common to all the stories are part of the genre, so you will want to include them in your story. Read fairy tales too, and don't limit yourself to Hans Christian Anderson and the Brothers

Grimm. Read Russian fairy tales, and Japanese ghost stories. Look into Native American folklore. Here is a wealth of material for the fledgling fantasy writer!

In every creative discipline, the end 'product' is the result of practice! practice! practice! Every successful book has gone through myriad drafts and revisions (rehearsing), and a few arguments with an editor (the audience/critic). No one just bangs out a good best-seller without these steps. Two questions resonate in the creative person's mind: 1) is this what I wanted? and 2) can I do this better?

Regardless of *what* you are writing, you have to know:

- yourself and how you want people to see you in this instance;
- what it is you want to say, and why;
- to whom you are speaking;
- when to stop.

Recently, a friend decided to write her life story, and showed me some of her early efforts. As far as I could tell, she hadn't answered most of these questions. I never knew what aspect of her Self was speaking. Was she a wise woman who had learnt much during her journey on Earth, or a tragic victim of a painful childhood? Was the reader meant to see her as a hero, a philosopher, or a psycho?

A mistake that many neo-writers make is forcing a 'writing style'—trying to write in the manner of someone they have read. Can you imagine a book like

'The Man in the Iron Mask' if it had been written by AA Milne, or 'The Velveteen Rabbit' by Alexander Solzhenitsyn? The writing style of an author is the result of considerable growth and maturation, plenty of rehearsal, and a willingness to look critically within and accept this can be better (until, of course, it can't be).

Good writing is the fruit of humility; bad writing is a source of humiliation.

So, here you are. You know who you are; you know what information or tale you want to relate; you have an idea how to cause readers to be most receptive. You know your subject. You know *why* you want to tell this particular tale. The computer is on, your coffee is at hand, your story is mapped out, and you're feeling very 'authorly'. What comes next?

BALANCE. Pick a starting point. Write down the basic elements of what you want to say. When you've done that, leave the room.

That's hard to do. Some perfectly wonderful tales have become perfectly dreadful writings because:

- the author was too descriptive;
- the author wasn't descriptive enough;
- the author wasn't informative enough;
- the author didn't know when to stop.

After reading the latest work of a best-selling author, I checked the reviews posted by fellow library-goers and was gratified that we all agreed on one particular point: the author missed at least half a dozen good opportunities to end his book, and as such, it dragged on forever.

Similarly, I read a book about whales that was so stunningly written that after I put it down I didn't want to pick it up again. The author wrote beautiful and detailed descriptions—so beautiful and so detailed, in fact, that the book was difficult to read and understand. The experience was akin to eating too much rich food too fast.

I imagine many people think a story 'simply flows' from the writer's pen, when in fact it must be built, almost in the same way you would build a house. You need plans, your materials and tools, you have to know how long it is meant to be, and who is going to read it.

Follow the outline you've set for yourself; you've researched the story; you know what you want to say. Say it. Come back later and look it over. Now you can start getting 'artsy' with it—lay down some descriptions, embellish some sentences, editing as you go along. Eventually you'll have a finished draft. (Oh bother, all that work and we still aren't done? No.)

When you've completed a draft, read it over to yourself, and read it **out loud**. You'll be surprised, as you listen to yourself, how wonderful certain passages sound, and how awful others do. Some sentences simply won't *feel* right, and you should pay attention to that feeling. As you listen to yourself, you'll catch the over-usage of words and phrases, another thing that can kill good writing. (I once gave a lecture at a university, and in my final preparations discovered I had used the same word six times on one page!) This will help you refine your writing.

In the beginning of this article I mentioned the importance of an outline. Some writers view this as crucial, while others prefer to 'let the book write itself,' which also can be very useful, depending on how inspired you feel. Both approaches have validity, but in my experience, a combination of the two has been most satisfying. A dedicated writer will view the outline as a guideline. Feel free to experiment and play with words and ideas—sometimes you can be inspired by your own creativity. Don't hesitate to change your storyline, or write more than one version of a scene to see which plays out best. Flexibility is as important as discipline in any creative field, and the more flexible you are, the more satisfying your creation will be.

One more thing—creativity depends on practice! practice! practice! Do your best to write every day, even if the end result of a day's exercise ends up in the rubbish bin. It gets easier as you go along, and your skills and talents will be honed and refine.

You have the technology, you have the facts. You can build your story and make it better. You may earn $6 million, so *get out there and write!*

Hello, Control! Are you there?
5 February 2014

Many people are obsessed with the idea of CONTROL. Since this is my fourth effort to write this article, I suspect I might be one.

Control is natural, just as having a temperature is natural, so long as that temperature is somewhere around 98.6F. When your body temperature exceeds 98.6F, then you have a fever, a headache and a problem. The same is true of control.

Within limits, control is a good thing. The only person you can control is yourself. Natural 'self-regulation' or 'self-mastery' insists that you are responsible for yourself. So, if during a hunting party, you lose control of your temper and start swearing at the bear you are tracking (let's say), don't be surprised when a) the others in your hunting party desert you and b) the bear eats you.

I confess strongly biased views regarding the *control of others*. In this I certainly am NOT alone. Very worthwhile social projects have been hindered, even ruined, because an agency insisted on trying to control, regulate and direct the professional environment, going so far as to tell unrelated agencies what they could and could not do. A friend was denied a very promising career in medicine because her father insisted she work in his business. There was no second choice. (Control always limits options.) More than one person has been institutionalized because no one thought a physically disabled person could live independently in the community. (They have been proven wrong *many* times.)

Despite my bias, I believe that *some* control is natural and necessary. Control is understood in relationships in which each party has a role to play. The supervisor is the captain of the ship; that parent makes the decisions; the kid with the ball plays, or takes his ball and goes home.

Control is also a function of ability—you speak French much better than I, we're in Paris, you order dinner for us both. The captain of the ship defers to the navigator, whose job it is to know how to get from place A to place B.

The *abuse* of control stems from distrust of others, lack of confidence in their abilities/integrity/character, and is a reaction to feelings of vulnerability. When one feels out of control, the inclination is to try and control everything else, often with destructive and even self-destructive results.

Many years ago I had a Board President who couldn't control a cough, let alone a Board of Directors. When she was unsure of her facts, she made them up. She made demands that could not be fulfilled, and flouted organizational philosophy when it suited her. The more she 'controlled', the less capable she was, and the less effective the rest of us were.

Some types of control are very obvious. The man with the badge tells you 'no', and you have no choice. That is a principle feature of control—your choices are limited or eliminated. If you don't let kid with the ball in the game, he *will* take his ball and go home, and you will have no game. The other kids may resent you for it, too. You can be managed by your fear of ostracism. However you respond, you are responsible for the outcome.

Judgement and criticism are means of controlling others. A psychologist once opined that many 'authority figures' (he was talking about parents) do this to express caring, because they want the best for their children, employees, etc. But a child who grows up thinking s/he isn't good enough becomes an adult who thinks s/he isn't good enough. The supervisor who never is satisfied with the work of the team ends up with a depressed and defeated team. What intrigues me is that, in my experience, the judgemental and critical person generally is uninformed on the subject. The idea seems to be, 'We will hire experts so we can ignore them.'

One of the subtlest forms of abuse of control is *Indecision*. I had a supervisor whose standard response was a variation of 'Well, I'm not sure about that', sometimes with comical results. In meetings, little was accomplished because we ended without a sense of finality—he wasn't sure, or didn't know, can because of this, we moved on with difficulty or not at all. There was also a colleague who, to make us think he was smarter than we, liked to respond 'Not necessarily!' to everything we said. Because they would not take a stand, no one else could take a stand either. We were manipulated by their indecision.

If control is about limiting options of others and forcing outcomes, control also requires taking responsibility for limiting options. Persuasion requires confidence and trust in others, and allows the relinquishing of responsibility to those better equipped to handle it. Some of the most persuasive discussions I've ever heard never ended, 'this is what you must do,' but left the decision to the listener. The persuasion was in the content. The persuader trusted the listener's judgement.

When others are encouraged to see your point of view, acknowledge your need(s), and ultimately *choose* to do what you have requested, your trust and confidence in them are implied. We do this every time we go to a restaurant, take our automobiles for servicing, or hire someone to build us something. The results are more positive and satisfactory.

Control or persuasion?

> *We may convince others by our arguments; but we can only persuade them by their own.*
> *Joseph Joubert:* Pensées

⁙

Valentine's Day
13 February 2014

The Day of celebrated Romance is upon us again! It's a shame a) it is so commercialized, and b) its *meaning* is so *under*-celebrated. Every day should be Valentine's Day. We should never let pass an opportunity to say the three most important words in a human's experience: I Love You.

The poets, of course, have made quite a foray into conveying the 'finer emotion', from 'Roses are Red', to odes of undetermined length. Robert Burns gives a fine example of good expression:

A Red Red Rose

O, my love is like a red, red rose,
That's newly sprung in June.
O, my love is like the melody,
That's sweetly played in tune.

As fair art thou, my bonnie lass,
So deep in love am I,
And I will love thee still, my dear,
Till all the seas gang dry.

Till all the seas gang dry, my dear,
And the rocks melt with the sun!
I will love thee still, my dear,
While the sands o' life shall run.

And fare thee well, my only love!
And fare thee well, a while!
And I will come again, my love,
Tho it were ten thousand mile!

You can sense the immense joy and pride this sturdy Scot takes in his bonnie lass, and his good fortune to have found her!

The Elizabethan Robert Herrick wrote many poems to cherished ladies. Scholars believe most, if not all of them, never existed. This is sad; Herrick certainly was overflowing with love.

To Electra

I dare not ask a kiss,
I dare not beg a smile,
Lest having that, or this,
I might grow proud the while.

No, no, the utmost share
Of my desire shall be
Only to kiss that air
That lately kissèd thee.

When you read this poem, you understand why he died a bachelor. A kiss should be like a drink of heady, spicy wine; to be visited with something lukewarm and watered-down instead must be very disappointing. I knew a man who made such a dramatic production of giving his sweetheart a romantic kiss that, if he started on Sunday, he wouldn't actually come in for a landing until Wednesday, only to 'kiss the air that lately kissèd she', because by that time, she'd *gone*!

John Donne exuded affection and adoration. To-day I suppose a woman thus addressed would roll her eyes and mutter 'Smarm' under her breath.

Daybreak

Stay, O sweet, and do not rise!
The light that shines comes from thine eyes;
The day breaks not: it is my heart,
Because that you and I must part.
Stay! Or else my joys will die
And perish in their infancy.

And yet, who in love has not felt the anguish of separation from the cherished? Or counted the anxious hours, even minutes, until they can be again in one another's embrace? Does not love give even the gloomiest of days a luminescence we can attribute to nothing else?

I love the passion with which Mihri Hatun wrote:

At one glance
I loved you
With a thousand hearts.

To be so consumed by love must be the most joyous experience of the human being. I earnestly wish you well of it.

These days it isn't always possible or welcome to say 'I love you' to someone. Some people respond to the declaration of love with fear, or indifference. It doesn't fit into their Master plan; it isn't always 'convenient'; it might hurt. The real beauty of Love is that it doesn't require *you* to love *me*, for *me* to love *you*. My happiness is in my love for you. If you love me back, then there is twice the joy.

> *Who can look upon this face*
> *And doubt the touch of Divine Grace*
> *Who has adorned for all to see*
> *Thy countenance for love of thee?*
> *But perhaps, for love of men,*
> *This radiant bloom above the stem.*
> *Ne'er in life shalt thou behold*
> *Such love for thee so open told*
> *As in the eyes of them that see*
> *And worship God for love of thee.*
>
> *PTNC, 2009*

I wish you all the happiest S Valentine's Day!

✠✠✠

Why did You Say It Like That?
14 February 2014

What words you choose, how you phrase your ideas, depends on your audience, the nature of your information, and what impression you want to leave the listener. It is just as important in written communication as it is in speaking, and of course, the advantage of written communication is that you have time to experiment and play with words until you actually express what you mean the way you mean it.

You might like to think of this as 'painting a picture with words.' Putting aside the subject of word choice for the moment, imagine you wanted to do an oil painting of the local park. You've chosen your particular site. Now—is this a morning or afternoon scene? You'll choose your colours and direct your shadows differently for each. What season of the year is this? That will influence your colour choice even further. And then—what style? Do you want this painting to have a dreamy, almost surreal quality? Do you want it to be sharp like a photograph? Should it depress the viewer, or give good cheer?

In speaking and writing, you make similar choices to these, and for that you need a good command of the language. The best way to do that is to savour the works of other speakers and writers. This will help you broaden your vocabulary and style. Exposure to poetry will help you develop a sensitivity to phrasing (the *brushstrokes* of your verbal painting). The best way for me to demonstrate this is to give you some examples.

A man who courts a lady will make an impression if he tells her she's a 'looker'—probably a bad one. 'Looker' sounds like he is objectifying her, and at best, she will not believe him to be sincere. A man who tells a woman he thinks she's 'beautiful' makes a more positive impression because the choice of word implies respect and admiration.

When someone loses a job, the employer has a choice of saying, 'You're fired!', 'I'm going to have to let you go,' and 'I'd like you to take early retirement.' Each phrase has a different impact. 'You're fired!' is unquestionably hostile, and the employer's only regret is that the employee won't be around so he can fire him again. 'I'm going to have to let you go,' suggests regret, and 'early retirement' implies this is a *good* thing, I'm doing you a favour.

People who write résumés, whether their own or someone else's, are confronted with the difficulty of talking about their earlier jobs in a way that is attention-catching. To put it another way, people composing résumés are challenged to relate previous employment activities in a compelling fashion.

A young woman described her current job responsibility as 'tossing the garbage.' After her job coach modified this sentence, she was 'responsible for the removal of end-of-day non-essential work product.' Another client explained that he was 'responsible for the dissemination and circulation of inter- and extra-departmental communiques, including government-issued certificates, within the structure of a corporate environment.' He worked in the company mailroom.

In this way, you choose your words with regard to the result you want to have. When someone asks you, 'does this make my hips look big?' you may be accurate in saying, 'like all outdoors!' but you will convey the same general impression without offense if you answer, 'You have other things in your wardrobe that are more complimentary.'

If you've seen a fashion show, when the first model comes on the runway, your immediate *private* observation might be 'she looks like a walking cupcake,' but if you're the fashion reporter for the local newspaper, you will write, '*the model wore a retro-design dress of layered lace, with gay, cheerful colours and matching accessories.*'

You might remember a scene in one of the Indiana Jones movies in which Sean Connery unintentionally fired a machine gun at the tail of his own bi-plane. When Harrison Ford asked what happened, Connery answered, 'We've been hit.' It was factual, but phrased in a way that Connery was spared embarrassment. He chose an unorthodox approach to the truth.

The world thrives on these sensitive approaches. Prison guards are now Corrections Officers; stewardesses are Flight Attendants, and the guy or gal who delivers your mail is a Postal Carrier, not a mail man. The Department of War has become the Department of Defence. There are always other ways to say what you mean, each with its own effect.

As much of an opponent as I am to 'specialized language', and as hostile as I am to the loathsome practice of 'politically correct language,' I concede there is a real need for *intelligently* sensitive communication. We live in an age in which people are always looking for new ways to be insulted. One must speak or write carefully.

There are many languages in which a single word can mean two things we would translate into English differently. In Romani, for example, one word—*piav*—means both 'smoke' and 'drink'. The word *muj* means both 'face' and 'mouth'. The verb 'to eat' can mean 'to kiss.' Be delighted when a beautiful Roma lady whispers to you (through an unskilled translator) that she wants to eat your mouth—it means she wants to kiss you. (The source for this information is *Bury Me Standing*, by Isabel Fonseca, pp 56-58.)

Fortunately, the English language is so rich that any desired impression can be made given the tasteful combination of words and phrases. You can make yourself clearly understood by the words you choose, and by the approach you take.

So, let's eat!

Political? Yes! Correct? Hell no!
21 February 2014

Many of the blogs I've written have discussed one aspect or another of communication. I wanted to share observations and impressions about word choice, the shaping and phrasing of sentences to be more sensitive and persuasive, and at the same time, make readers aware of subtle methods of control and influence.

In a recent conversation, 'politically correct language' came up, and I thought I would give that subject some attention, to dissuade you from ever using it.

Politically Correct Language (PCL) is one of the most offensive and deceptive forms of address in the English language. It is intended to convey awareness, sensitivity, an acknowledgement of individuality and difference. Originally it was meant to avoid 'labelling', but the PCL terms became labels in their own right. It is very 'political' in the sense that you rephrase the way you express yourself to suit your audience. It is a license to air your prejudices in polite terms, and it is interesting to note that PCL phrases are coined and used by people to whom the phrases do not apply.

The message PCL actually sends is one of ignorance, fear, and exclusion. PCL is *very sterile and unfeeling.* In some instances, there's an undertone of snobbery. For example, I know many people who are 'minorities'—Black, Hispanic, Asian, etc. None of them *ever* refer to themselves as 'people of colour'. That's left to the Caucasian PCL-ers, who, in the US, are the *majority.* They succeed in creating an 'us-and-them' dynamic, which is where trouble begins. An interesting note: PCL-ers don't recognize they are people of colour as well—pink!

Somewhere in our primal past, we recognized difference as a matter of survival—'this one is not from my group and may be an enemy'. It came from a fear of losing one's life. To-day this distinction seems to stem from a fear of losing one's identity as an individual or a member of a particular class, and keeping that identity pure.

In some instances, pointing out differences seems rational. Men have oppressed and dominated women in many fields of endeavour for centuries (and sometimes still do). Why wouldn't a woman want special recognition because she is doing a job typically held by a male (and may be doing it better)? The most important thing, though, is not the gender of the individual, but can s/he do the job? (There are some jobs for which a woman is doubtlessly unqualified—male stripper, for example.)

These distinctions (male/female, black/white, able/disabled, etc) confuse and conceal the actual matters. Many years ago, a blind man sang a solo at a choral concert in Chicago. He sang off-key and his voice cracked, but he received a lengthy standing ovation. If he had not been blind, he would have been booed off the stage. Because he was blind, the audience showered him with accolades. With that 'standard' in place, all my readers should adore me and praise me for my excellence and genius, because I have *multiple physical disabilities.* (Let me add, if you do, you're a mug.)

Having been disabled all my adult life, and having worked in the field of disability most of my adult life, I've encountered numerous social workers trained to modern standards, both as a professional and as a client. These social workers are taught to be professional in their behaviour, and it carries over into, and contaminates, their communication. It desensitizes them to their clients. As I mentioned, PCL is *sterile*—there's no feeling behind it, no genuine commitment, no *honesty*. Whenever I heard PCL being used, I knew my client was in trouble. The social workers who did the best job, and who related best to their clients, took a no-nonsense approach and did not bother with fluffy language.

I have no problem identifying myself as a 'disabled person'. There are advocates in the disability community who say I should refer to myself as a 'person with a disability' because *my* way puts the disability before the person. It is a matter of personal choice which you use.

There are expressions that are considered pejorative in to-day's disabled society. 'Cripple' is an ugly word, connoting something sick, broken and useless. 'Handicap' originated in Elizabethan times when the disabled collected alms 'cap-in-hand'—we were drones and drains on polite society. 'Deaf-mute' and 'deaf and dumb' are expressions almost always inaccurate—I used to work with deaf people, none of whom were mute, nor stupid, but all of whom were offended at being referred to as 'deaf mute'. 'Halt', 'lame,' and 'maimed' aren't frequently used these days, but they are equally unwelcome.

I am not, nor have I heard any other disabled people call themselves, *physically challenged, differently abled, other-abled, having special needs,* and Lord strike me dead if anyone ever uses the expression *handi-capable* around me. We don't need the cute terminology PCL-ers have created for us. It's demeaning. My biggest 'physical challenge' is getting my grocery cart up a flight of iron stairs. I walk with a cane, I have lots of joint pain, and my sense of balance is poor. The same is true for many people my age. (I've been nine years old so many times over, I've lost count.)

PCL is *silly*. I was examined by a neurologist and I mentioned I have a history of Stiff Man's Syndrome. I was immediately corrected—it is now (officially) Stiff *Person* Syndrome. I asked her, since the original title to this very rare condition was Moersch Woltman Syndrome, would she prefer to refer to it as Moersch Woltperson Syndrome? She didn't see the humour.

Although I've referred a great deal to disability, these objections apply to PCL as used regarding race, gender, sexual preference, and many other areas of 'sensitivity'. PCL is based on the false assumption that PUUs (People Unlike Us) require special treatment, and even a special vocabulary. There are enough real disparities between us already. There are enough *genuine* wounds that need healing and sensitive handling. These realities make any degree of unity difficult. Artifices such as PCL fan the flames, and sometimes make matters considerably worse.

The differences are already clear enough. Why not say what you mean, and embrace the similarities?

✢✢✢

Credo
27 February 2014

This weekend past, I volunteered at a Youth Art Fair, sponsored by the local Art League. It was a very enjoyable day, filled with pleasant sights and people, interesting conversation (and of course, enough material for at least two blogs!) Volunteering felt good, and I was rewarded for my time with two outstanding moments.

The first was when a friend—a very talented artist and award-winning silversmith—explained to me how the artwork of kindergarten and nursery school children is evaluated by the judges. I could see only shapes and blobs. She showed me favourable characteristics a judge might look for in several pictures that had been contributed by the 'under sixes'. This child filled the background with uniform strokes of her crayon, all going in the same direction—she didn't scribble it in. That child didn't use primary colours, thus giving the watercolour picture of a flower an appealing and gentle appearance. Another child had actually mixed media—tiny blossoms glued onto a branch painted in sumi-e ink. All these artists were under the age of five.

In less than sixty seconds, she opened my eyes to something I would never have otherwise been able to grasp! (This new vision humbled me too; I walked away realizing you will get more money for a Vermeer done at age 3 than you will for a Chapman done at age 59!)

The second moment came during the award ceremony. The exhibits were arranged by the school grade of the artist. I was responsible for bringing forward the 1st prize-winning artwork for each grade. The children sat near their artwork, waiting for 'the envelope please'. When I approached a table to retrieve one particular student's first-prize artwork, the artist (age 11?) saw me approach, and his eyes widened in surprise. He watched me pick up his picture and an enormous smile spread across his face as he realized he had won. I don't recall ever having seen such pure joy. It was a moment I won't forget.

A lot of children who brought their work to the school the morning of the show seemed to be hesitant, if not actually stunned—'*why am I doing this?*' After the award ceremony, when the exodus of parents, children and art pieces most resembled Napoleon's Retreat from Moscow, the children seemed happy and satisfied, even if they hadn't won a ribbon and a prize. Just being at the art fair had given them a sense of accomplishment—'I *can* do this!'

For the rest of the weekend, I thought about creativity in general terms. It requires more than the ability to draw, or create an image with words or sounds. The Arts are meant not only to entertain and soothe, but to challenge and surprise us as well. I thought about what goes into 'being creative'.

Well, naturally, you have to have *imagination*. That generates *ideas*. You need the ability to express those ideas, which calls on *vision* and *innovation*. *Talent* is a good thing to have, of course, and after a while, you will need a lot of that four-letter word—*discipline*.

None of this matters if you lack the ingredient that holds all the rest together—*belief in yourself*. If you don't think you can succeed, you won't. A defeatist attitude invariably guarantees a defeated attempt.

There is a 'hidden benefit' to art fairs, writing competitions, dance recitals and the school play. Sure, the children have an opportunity to showcase their work, and the parents to beam with pride and tell everyone, '*My* kid did that!' These events offer people an opportunity to believe in themselves. That is a very daring thing, for children and adults alike. Up to now, creativity has been a personal, private thing, and now the whole world will see it.

It's paradoxical that individual belief is a *community* effort. Positive individuality thrives in a positive, nurturing environment. You can't get figs from thistles, we're told. Even more paradoxical, individual belief in one's self may *start with someone else*. The seed of potential already exists, but it must be planted, watered and nourished. Few people are strong enough to maintain belief in self in the midst of an environment of doubt and disbelief.

This poses a challenge to all of us. Positive, supportive environments are difficult to discover and to maintain. The media, the small and silver screens, are replete with examples of disbelief, scorn, and derision. I'm certain we all remember moments in our lives that were painful and disastrous, primarily because of the negative and defeating attitudes of the people around us. The challenge is to create enough positive environments in the world, thus allowing all sorts of creativity to flourish because people believe in themselves and each other.

I'm very glad there are Youth Art Fairs, Poetry Competitions, Amateur Dramatic Societies, and even the local church choir concert. They offer artists and performers an opportunity. On the face of it, they all say: *show us what you can do.*

The vital subtext is this: *we believe in you.*

✢✢✢

The Lost Art
6 March 2014

Recently one of my facetube friends 'liked' on her page a post about listening, which reminded me that listening is one critical component of communication I've never discussed. (Perhaps I wasn't paying attention!)

It started me thinking about listening.

I was a psychology major at university in the 1970's, when the field was overrun with 'psychobabble'. People 'heard what you're saying', or 'resonated to that.' They 'felt your pain' as they pondered 'the reality of the situation'. (Sheesh!) A professor of clinical psychology actually *instructed* her classes on how to listen:

Sit with your shoulders back and relaxed, cradle your hands in your lap. Maintain eye contact—crinkle your eyes a little. Tilt your head a bit to one side, nod as the other person speaks, and respond vocally from time to time. Say nothing judgemental or critical—respond with 'I hear you,' (or if it's not too early in the morning and you can manage multisyllabic words) 'uh-huh'. Try to put the other person at ease.

The end result was a bunch of squinty-eyed psychology majors with wry neck, bearing a striking resemblance to a bobble-head doll.

I think about some of the good listeners I've known in my life, and what it was about them that made them such good listeners.

For one thing, they were completely natural—none of the posing mentioned above. They listened with appropriate respectfulness. Conversations that are more like sparring are not an uncommon experience for anyone—you say about four words, and the person to whom you are speaking jumps in with a quip or comment. Good breeding insists that you respond to that remark before continuing. It happens again and again, and you may well forget what it is you were trying to convey. Such conversations are wearisome.

These listeners actually *listened.* They maintained eye contact, they stood in one place so I wasn't talking to a moving target, and they didn't interrupt. Their faces showed they were interested, as did their comments and follow-up questions.

Body language practically screams during the act of listening, and the good listeners behave naturally; the expression on their faces and the (un)relaxed manner in which they hold their bodies will certainly tell you if you're getting through to them. They maintain eye contact, but not of the 'deer in the headlights' variety. It would be natural, at a party for example, to look around the room from time to time, but the people I'm thinking of devote their 'eye-attention' primarily to the speaker.

Listening is ironically an *expressive* part of communication. How a person listens says a great deal—regard, investment in the other person, interest, and response.

While I know some very good listeners, I know some dreadful listeners as well. For example, while you are talking, they nod their heads and say, 'yes, yes', at about four times the normal rate. They give the impression of listening faster than you are speaking. Those who interrupt constantly seem to be trying to control the conversation. Perhaps they think they are participating or showing enthusiasm, but such fractured conversations are difficult and frustrating to tolerate. I mentioned the 'moving target' earlier—when I encounter one of these, I feel utterly superfluous.

A good listener will not make you repeat yourself. I'm thinking at the moment of a woman whose first response invariably was 'What?' even when all you said was, 'Good morning, how are you?' Some of her contemporaries, instead of saying 'what?' honked 'huh?' I do not miss those days.

I'm also thinking about a priest I knew a long time ago. Of all the priests in his parish, he was the one most sought-after for confessions. This wasn't because he gave the lightest penances, or even the best advice. It was because he was the best listener in the bunch, and when you left the confessional, you felt you had left many weighty burdens behind. Contrast this to one of his associate pastors, whose sermons were reminiscent of a plane endlessly circling the airport for a landing. Will Rogers should have taught at his seminary: *Never miss a good chance to shut up.*

I suppose the thing that impresses me the most about good listeners is a tacit understanding that a conversation, like a plant, a relationship or a promise, is a 'living' thing. It needs attention, nurturing, and respect. People who spend long periods in isolation appreciate this all too well. It isn't enough to have someone to talk to; you need someone to actually *heed* you.

A common complaint is, 'he never shuts up!' I've never heard anyone say, 'what a terrible conversation! All she did was listen!'

> *"The most basic of all human needs is the need to understand and be understood. The best way to understand people is to listen to them."*
> — Ralph G. Nichols

※

My Love Affair with Fountain Pens
14 March 2014

I always write with a fountain pen—a proper writing instrument with a nib, filled from a bottle. People often ask why, because in this day and age of throw-away everything, a fountain pen seems like a throw-back item. There are always remarks, but happily, they are remarks of admiration and approval.

I acquired my first fountain pen at the age of ten, when I served a year of scholastic servitude in a private school. It was an Osmiroid pen with an Italic nib, filled from a bottle of Pelikan black ink. Our history master had decided that what stood for penmanship in public schools was crap (his word), and undertook to teach us Chancery Cursive, which I believe had its origins in Elizabethan times. It was a very interesting and attractive style of writing, but in the 20th century, impractical because to be done properly, you had to *draw* each letter. And, properly done, it pretty much eliminated the individual characteristics of personal penmanship. It was best written with a fountain pen and italic nib, and that's what started me down the road of something special.

When I was thirteen, I bought myself a Parker 75, which saw me through high school and university. If the Osmiroid was a calligrapher's tool, the Parker was the tool of a sincere scholar. Now I use a Pelikan or an Aurora, always filled from a bottle; these are the indispensable instruments of a serious writer.

Writing with a fountain pen is the beginning of a creative process. If you have a good pen (and from here on out, when I say 'pen', I mean *fountain* pen), you treat it with respect. You clean it, fill it with a good quality ink, and are sure to wipe the nib. The nibs of the pens are soft enough to yield to the pressure of the writer's hand, lending expression and character to the lines. If you press hard, the lines are broader, and you develop a sense for controlling the flow of ink. The pen introduces an element of self-expression. It is a tacit statement of the commitment and thoughtfulness in your writing. The pen aids a sincere intellect.

When you decide to write, your pen helps you 'get into the mind-set' you want. People kneel and fold their hands when they pray; in wooing your sweetheart, you light candles, put on soft music, and set out a bottle of good wine. The tone is set, a mood is created. Picking up the pen invokes a creative atmosphere within you. You are about to put your thoughts and feelings on paper for all to see. You will be careful, deliberate, and you will express yourself fully and sincerely. It will show, not only in your choice of words, but in your handwriting as well.

Too often, in this modern day and age, we sacrifice elegance and sophistication in favour of convenience. When your ball point, or your cigarette lighter, runs out its 'vital fluid', throw it away and get a new one. Electronics now are manufactured such that when they break down, you can just throw them away and buy a replacement—they are not constructed to be repaired. Few products to-day really require much in the way of care and up-keep. This is a sad thing; when the capacity for care and conservation begins to wane in small things, it will eventually wane in greater things as well.

Naturally, every implement has its appropriate use. You would no more need a fountain pen to write your shopping list than you would a sable-hair paint brush. Modern 'throw-aways' are fine for that. The modern writing utensil, the ball/roller/gel pen, lacks these necessary creative qualities—to me, they aren't much more expressive than something typewritten or printed on a laser printer. Would you write a love letter on a typewriter or computer? Certainly not!

It's impossible for me to feel any affection for the ball point and its cousins, the gel and roller ball pens. The lines are uniform and lacking in character, the ink clots, and there is a distinct lack of warmth or character in the visual presentation. These pens are fine for signing cheques, for drafting, or dashing off a note to your milkman. I can think of no finer emergency beer can opener than a ball point rammed through the top of the can a couple of times. You need a tracheostomy—the sort they show on those television dramas? By all means, snap my Bic Stick in half, and uses the barrel to create an airway!

You wouldn't do that with a fountain pen.

✤✤✤

The Lost Art—Part Two
14 March 2014

Last week end, I was given a wonderful gift. Someone told me about an experience she'd had recently. I listened to her observations and opinions, and expressed my support. When she finished, she said, 'Thank you for listening.'

Later in the same afternoon, I watched a DVD from Britain, and in the course of scripted conversation, Party A thanked Party B for listening. They are apparently very polite in Britain—this happened two or three times in a single episode.

What is it about listening that is so special that when you do listen, people feel you should be thanked? It can't be simply good manners. There's something more that compels gratitude and appreciation in people (or so it seems to me).

People usually don't talk TO one another; they talk AT each other. Even when they hear you, they often don't listen. It's almost worse than being overtly ignored.

Listening is a wonderful and unappreciated activity—I love to listen. It's rewarding and enriching. When someone shares an experience, a feeling or an idea, I feel privileged and honoured. I am engaged, and for a moment, I am part of the other person's life, even if only as an observer. Listening is an effortless way of expressing care, or love. (It is effortless in that it requires nothing *from* you, but it can also be very difficult. It sometimes takes a lot of effort to say NOTHING.)

We know from experience that it is a beautiful feeling to be heard. In the previous article on listening, I mentioned a priest who was very popular as a confessor because he was such a good listener. When parishioners discussed worries or problems with him, they felt unburdened, or at the very least, they felt understood by the time the conversation was over.

I also worked with a psychiatrist who, during his sessions with clients, sat with his feet up on his desk and his eyes closed as the client sat across from him and tried to talk, usually to his wing-tip shoes. I attribute his therapeutic success to the astute use of psychotropic medications; it is doubtful counselling had much to do with it. (His receptionist was a much better listener than he.)

Confiding in people isn't always comfortable, no matter how well you might know them. What you have to say may be a delicate subject, deeply personal, very negative, or possibly be upsetting to the person to whom you want to speak. When a person in that situation chooses to share, s/he may feel s/he is taking a huge risk. (And to be blunt, if s/he FEELS s/he is taking a risk, then s/he IS taking a risk.)

What does this risk entail? People dislike exposing vulnerabilities, being seen as sick, weak, or foolish. What they have to tell may make them appear ignorant, irrational, or immoral. That may be the principle concern that makes talking so difficult. People who share something personal are hoping for support and validation—are hoping for it and deserve it. Judgement and brutal criticism have no place.

I worked with a man who judged and criticized everything I said or did; he thought I craved his approval. I was so damaged and undermined by his constant negativity and critical commentary that I became unable to function, and was greatly relieved when we finally parted company. My feelings were validated when I confided to someone else that I did not trust this first individual, and was told, 'Neither do I.'

I understand why being open with another person is risky. I remember vividly how much it hurt to feel vulnerable and have that vulnerability taken advantage of. I also remember how great it is to have support—the man who said, 'Neither do I' will never know the full extent of his effect on me. It felt fantastic to be heard—to receive intelligent and responsive replies to my comments and confidences. I feel restored when someone agrees with me or supported me.

It is thrilling to be confided in—I relish the trust, appreciate the risk, enjoy the richness of a shared (if only second-hand) experience in someone else's life. I feel I've been given a gift being healed when someone says, 'Thank you for listening to me.'

I wonder why it's such an unusual thing.

Many of the blogs and articles we read these days are negative, critical, and destructive. In any instance of notoriety, you can look on facetube and read angry and irrational reactions to a devastating event, usually heavily laden with misrepresentation and misunderstanding. There is enough negativity in the world already.

It is time to heal.

Listen.

The Book—A Feast in Words
20 March 2014

I would like to talk about how a story in book form is 'constructed'. In a previous article, I mentioned that stories do not simply FLOW from the author's pen, and actually, the best books begin as simple thoughts, and are repeatedly revisited, fine-tuned, honed and embellished. Thus, the nightmare you had last Wednesday and only vaguely remember, can become a modern-day *War and Peace* given time, care and attention.

Lewis Carroll's King, in *Alice's Adventures in Wonderland* put it best: *'Begin at the beginning…and go on till you come to the end: then stop.'* It's often easier to write the more exciting and interesting bits first, but there's no avoiding it—no story can exist without Chapter One.

The beginning of a book is one of the most challenging parts to write because it strongly influences whether the reader will bother to move on to Chapter Two. Chapter One must establish the setting and nature of the book, introduce basic concepts, feature at least one character, and create a foundation on which the rest of the book will be based. It must be neither so boring nor so overly informative that the gentle reader wants to shuffle off to wash dishes rather than digest your magnum opus.

All books have this problem. At university, a psychology professor said of his own text book, 'first chapters are always boring, even mine.' A Great Tale must have a Great Beginning, capturing the reader's interest and whetting the appetite for what is to come.

As a writer, it's a good idea to have at least roughed out the final chapter as well. It helps to develop and shape the story, a sort of 'destination' for your narrative journey. The end of a story has a second element of challenge. Some writers fail to provide a sufficiently exhilarating conclusion, and others finish too quickly. Some conclude their stories with something so esoteric that only they get the point. Others miss half a dozen opportunities to conclude, and leave the reader feeling s/he is endlessly circling the drain.

Now you know the beginning and the end. With the tedious bits behind you, the real fun begins—you get to write the middle. The first and last chapters are anchors. In the middle, you can do anything and go anywhere you like with your story. This is the part with the greatest flexibility, the greatest potential for exploration and experimentation, and the greatest room for imagination.

Writing a book is like hosting a magnificent banquet, and reading a book is like attending one. Chapter One is the Appetizer—it needs to taste good, but not be so filling there's no room for the rest of the dinner. It's meant to stimulate your appetite so you stick around for the fish and macaroni, instead of grabbing your hat and saying, 'Must run!'

The other dishes in the feast fill and satisfy the most, and the courses offered complement each other. If you begin by offering shrimp puffs, crab cakes and pate, the next dish shouldn't be a Sloppy Joe. Within that framework between first and last courses, myriad suitable options offer themselves and wait only to be chosen.

So it is with writing of the rest of the book. Experiment with characters and approaches to a particular point. Give your imagination free rein—sometimes the momentum of a single creative thought can carry you for chapters. Try to have multiple options from which to select the most appropriate and fitting continuation for your story, and for Heaven's sake, have fun with it! People will only see what you publish, feel free to be silly. But do be consistent. In biographies, while it might make sense to write about the subject's parentage, no one will be particularly interested until they've met the subject of the biography. The family tree can follow, but must not lead.

To conclude the banquet analogy: the last course is dessert, and if the dinner has been interesting and satisfying, the dessert should be too. My personal preference for a sweet, like a small sorbet, is rightly overruled by gateau, pie a la mode, or something soaked in brandy and set on fire.

Like the banquet, the book has to come to a conclusion; there has to be a dramatic (or at least interesting) event to bring the story to a close. A story that ends, 'and they all went home' is likely to leave the reader feeling unsatisfied. Therefore, you can write that He, who has yearned for She for ages, finally has worked up the courage to seize Her in his arms and, at long last, cover her pretty, upturned face with hot, burning kisses.

There's no need to mention the restraining order that follows.

So, dear friends, welcome to the Feast!

✢✢✢

Send the Marines
23 March 2014

Before I relocated to American Siberia, I used to frequent a cigar lounge, not surprisingly located inside a large cigar store, in the East. This was at a time when I was brutalized by the malice, viciousness, and outright dishonesty of people I had thought were my friends, and I've struggled with post-traumatic stress ever since.

Going to this cigar lounge helped me a long way in the early days of my efforts to recover. When I entered the store, someone greeted me, often by name, and sometimes someone even patted my shoulder or shook my hand. I'm not ashamed to say the first time this happened, I cried. Normalcy is a wonderful healer, especially when it is constant.

The men who frequented this lounge were from various professional, educational, cultural and religious backgrounds. The conversations ranged from instructive to hilarious, matter of fact to profound. It was often difficult to leave at the end of my day.

Among the smoky throng of smoking men was a small group I would like to talk about to-day. They were former Marines (there is no such thing as an 'ex-Marine'). They seemed to project a strength and sense of self-discipline that I envy. Several of these gentlemen (and they WERE Gentlemen) had been snipers in Afghanistan and Iraq, and not surprisingly, suffered from PTSD. They never talked with each other about battles or missions—the horrors were instantly understood. They did sometimes discuss places they'd been (I learnt that in one of Saddam's palaces, he had a solid gold toilet, which is grist for many jokes about the economy, I'm sure), and how they were doing now.

As I observed these men, it was easy to see that, even though they might have just met, there was a bond between them. They were brothers in arms, with disparate yet shared experiences. There was no doubt in my mind that in an instant, they would have each other's backs, regardless of the crisis.

I envied them their camaraderie.

Their PTSD was another bond between them. They talked about their experiences in muted tones, not to hide their own difficulties, but to respect the privacy of the other fellow. It was one more common experience.

And because they recognized that I had PTSD too, they made me, for a time, part of their brotherhood. I was never too-something, overly-something else, or inadequate in other ways. I just was. They received me with warmth, compassion and understanding, and it was amazing to me that they accepted me at all. They had known real battlefields. One gentleman said to me, 'In the Marines, I had to do things of which I am thoroughly ashamed and for which I will spend the rest of my life trying to atone.' I can't imagine living with so great a burden. In comparison to them, my trauma was a flea bite, but they thought no less of me or my experience.

One does not imagine the military being compassionate or particularly caring. We hear about battles, numbers of deaths, and we've become familiar with the names of lethal weapons like IEDs or RPGs. In meeting these men, however, it is difficult to imagine that one could NOT feel tremendous respect and even admiration for them and the many others like them.

There are very few times or places for which I feel any nostalgia, but I miss that cigar lounge and its smoky throng of smoking men. I miss the Marines. They personified so well the Marine motto, *Semper Fi*.

Always faithful.

✦✦✦

Preparing for the Interview
25 March 2014

In another time, in another galaxy, interviews were simple things. This bloke went and talked to that bloke. That bloke gave a job to This bloke. They shook hands. Happiness and smiles all around.

Now, according to some experts, interviewing for a job will take anywhere from four to six 'meetings', conducted by telephone or via video conference as well as in person. (At a conference I attended last week, I heard of a man who was interviewed by nine different people for the position for which he was finally hired.) No one actually makes the decision alone.

These experts offer advice on how to prepare for a job interview, and the range of their advice goes from reasonable to ludicrous. One expert gave his clients such a detailed (and extreme) list of preparatory steps that it sounded as if he were teaching how to conduct a daring daylight bank robbery. He also advised making friends with the department receptionist, because her input might be the 'decisive factor', and, if offered a beverage, to take it in your LEFT hand, when shaking hands keep yours PERPENDICULAR to the floor, and don't cross your legs.

Ah.

Certain steps are obvious. Take a bath, shave where appropriate, wear clothing. Try not to smell (no cologne, no smoking until after the interview). Show up on time. Dress appropriately for the position you are seeking. If you are applying for a house-keeping position, do not show up in a Saville Row suit; if you are applying to be bank president, cut-offs and flip-flops are not recommended.

There are valid things to do to make ready: research the company as best you can. Find out as much as you can about the business, the corporate culture, institutional philosophies, etc. Try to know something about the competition (although there are not competitors in every profession).

Read your resume thoroughly. There's nothing more awkward in an interview than being questioned about something you've forgotten you said because you've rewritten your CV so many times. (In fact, to save yourself difficulty, take copies of your current CV with you, and offer it as an 'update'. And read it thoroughly before you do.)

Let this be your mantra: BE POSITIVE IN EVERYTHING. Even when presenting negative information, do it in in honest and positive way. That two-year period of unemployment can be presented as a 'time-out opportunity to reassess your priorities, acquire additional training and information, and make decisions about the course in life you wish to pursue. Now you're seeking opportunities to make contributions in <whatever>.'

I advise embracing a different mental attitude from those of other candidates. The situation is that you need a (different) job; that's usually foremost in most interviewees' thinking. Forget about that for the moment. All the other candidates want/need a job too; you'll hardly stand out in the crowd. Instead of thinking about what you want or need, think about the interviewer's needs instead.

You're about to be interviewed by someone who has his own set of problems and needs. This person has been tasked with identifying suitable candidates for a position the bosses have created. S/he may conduct only the first interview. You have to be memorable to be recommended for further consideration.

In the preliminary interview, the issue most concerning the interviewer (really) is not if you know how to tune pipe organs, or can reduce mint jelly without burning it, but if in a general way, you're a person who might 'fit in' to the bigger picture. Questions from the interviewer might SEEM to show an interest in you, but actually are part of a check list—can you tune a pipe organ? can you reduce mint jelly? do you have a match? what time is it in Zurich?

People love to be LISTENED TO, so as the interviewer takes you through your paces, ask open ended questions when you can, elicit information from her and LISTEN. (An open ended question is one that cannot be given a one-word answer such as 'yes' or 'no'.) Use the information you are given to focus your answers and be more responsive to the interviewer's need.

People remember stories much better than they do lists of facts. They enjoy stories—they're entertaining and don't require the brain-drain that a list of facts does. Prepare stories to illustrate your accomplishments, and here's a tip I was given recently: let the first line of your story be true but outrageous: 'Oh yes, I saved my last department $240 thousand using a thumb tack.' That's memorable. Now back it up with facts, limit of three—more tend to make the interviewer's eyes glaze over. Then, finish with a very positive statement that really just repeats (in different words) the things you just said. You will be remembered.

Present everything in as positive a fashion as possible. Significant personal problems such as death and divorce can be represented briefly as 'changes in my personal life,' and leave it at that. Were you dismissed from your last position, or did you take advantage of the opportunity to explore and pursue alternative interests?

Another suggestion—DON'T ask for the job. People do not like to be sold to (and in a job interview, you're trying to sell the idea that you're the answer to all their problems). They do not like being told what to do. They like to make their own decisions; when they make a decision, they own it and they're invested in it. So don't tell them 'You want to hire me. I'm the best person for the job.' You're forcing yourself on them.

Instead, demonstrate how you handle situations based on past experience, offer forward-looking ideas for the future, and maintain the mental attitude that you're there in that meeting room to help the interviewer solve the problem of finding suitable candidates. Conclude by saying, 'I'd be interested in pursuing this.' Instead of forcing yourself on the interviewer, you're leaving the unpressured opportunity for the interviewer to think, 'this person should be put forward as a candidate.'

Because of your stories with the true and outrageous first lines, you'll be remembered. Because you were helpful and supportive to the interviewer in the quest to find a suitable candidate, you'll be warmly appreciated. When the time comes, you'll stand out from the crowd as memorable and different, focused and positive. You more probably will be proposed for additional interviews than the other candidates.

In the end, you're the one everyone sees as the 'go-to' person for your field.

The 'Go-To' folks are the ones that get hired.

✥✥✥

Appreciating Appreciation
31 March 2014

A couple of weeks ago, a gentleman in Tennessee said something to me that opened my eyes and made me think about something that is with us all the time, but yet we never see.

I had sent him a tobacco pipe for repair, and if I liked the job he did, I had a larger repair project for him. He did an excellent job—I couldn't imagine it being done better—and I called him to tell him so. When we'd finished our conversation, he said something no one has ever said to me before.

Most of the time, we are told, 'thanks, I appreciate it,' and it's really a polite brush-off phrase. One can never be sure whether this 'brush off' is an expression of modesty, or just a matter of negligence. Complements and congratulations often are given as a matter of course, and are expressed so often that they've lost their meaning. 'Thank you', 'I'm sorry', 'take care', and my personal bête noire, the waiter's meaningless refrain, 'Enjoy!'—do they actually *mean* this, or is this noise to fill a silence?

The man in Tennessee said something that could only be intentionally forthright: 'Thank you, I appreciate YOU.'

We don't sincerely express ourselves to others often enough. Statements of affection and gratitude we may utter have become elisions of meaning and not expressions of feeling. I know the waiter who just brought me my lunch isn't really too concerned whether I enjoy my skirt steak or not, so long as I pay the bill, and the person for whom I've just done a favour probably didn't give the act a second thought when s/he said, 'I appreciate it.' (Actually, ''preciate it.')

When you mess up, be sure the world is not going to overlook it. You will hear about it for a long time. If you mess up or do something 'outside the box' publicly enough, you can be sure your detractors will be vocal, even if they didn't understand what it is you did.

If you do something right or praiseworthy, you may well find yourself wondering if anyone noticed.

It would be wonderful if people were more vocal and thoughtful about their positive feelings and attitudes. It would be really nice if 'take care' were a genuine expression of desire for your wellbeing, and not a cursive substitute for 'buzz off.' There is a responsibility behind such genuine utterances—don't say 'I'm sorry,' and then laugh at the misfortune. If you say 'I like you,' to someone, then treat that person with the friendliness and sincerity that 'liking someone' signifies. The words are meant to be the expression of the feeling.

In a former life, I presided at a number of memorial services, and talked with a lot of people about grief. One of the most frequent statements made was a variation on, 'I never told him....' It's quite likely, and very sad, that a large number of people go to their graves thinking they are unloved, disliked, or unappreciated, never knowing the truth. The truth is not meant to be a secret, but it often is, and lies are more common.

The world is not going to change because I said so. I do hope people will begin to consider what they say, how they mean it, and express themselves honestly, but I have no great anticipation.

I think it would be nice if people learnt to appreciate themselves. Recently a blog was posted in which the writer demonstrated a new skill, and then referred to his own efforts in the most insulting and degrading of terms. His efforts, actually, were quite good, and I wonder if his negativity put off readers who might like to have said, 'Hey, good job!'

Whereas you may donate blood and be told, 'Thanks, have a cookie and don't leave for half an hour,' consider what you've done—you've given something quite literally of yourself, and that will help someone else live. Appreciate that, and what that act of kindness says about you as a person. Let that help you grow. And be sincere in your appreciations—you may well be doing for yourself something others forgot to do.

'Appreciation is a wonderful thing. It makes what is excellent in others belong to us as well.' — *Voltaire*

✣✣✣

Creativity—In the Beginning...
5 April 2014

Taylor Swift was recently quoted as saying:

>*I'd like to think you don't stop being creative once you get happy.*

It isn't surprising that Ms Swift, who has earned many awards for her creativity, has spoken volumes in one brief insightful sentence.

George Bernard Shaw wrote: 'Imagination is the beginning of creation. You imagine what you desire, you will what you imagine, and at last, you create what you will.' Steve Jobs said: 'Creativity is just connecting things. When you ask creative people how they did something, they feel a little guilty because they didn't really do it, they just saw something. It seemed obvious to them after a while.'

I think Ms Swift was referring to something else, a different element of creativity that we all have within us, something a bit more profound.

Creativity is a response to a need, like a hunger. There must be hunger or there will be no feast. Looking at the early lives of many of our most creative poets, authors, painters, and musicians, we often see lives rife with sorrow and desolation. For example, Dorothy Parker, a very successful poet, satirist, and screenplay writer, struggled with abuse as a child, the death of her parents and step mother at an early age, and later, alcoholism, depression, and unsatisfactory relationships. It was the darkness of her life that shaped her creativity, which entertained others in the form of satire.

One of the most brilliant and imaginative writers in American literature was Edgar Allan Poe, whose life was riddled with sorrow, conflict, and self-destructive behaviours. No Pollyanna he who wrote 'The Raven', 'The Tell-tale Heart', and other macabre stories. Some of his most beautiful poetry was tinged by sorrow and the grave.

The Elizabethan poet Robert Herrick wrote many moving, beautiful love poems to a variety of ladies. Many scholars believe that few (perhaps none) of these women actually existed. It may have been that Herrick wished he had someone to love, or perhaps he was expressing in beautiful verse his desire for someone to love him.

Fantasy is a form of creation; it can be an end in itself, or the beginning of a much more productive effort. It is a desire for something better, or at least, something different. The human being always struggles to maintain a sense of balance. Something bad has happened, now something good must take place. From the ugliness of our past, beauty will arise. Fantasy can help us to achieve a sense of balance. The step after fantasy is creation.

This is not to say that in order to be creative, you *must* have led a tragic life; rather, many of the best creative souls seem to have come from heartrending beginnings. There may well be a highly creative musician, artist or writer whose life has been scarred by happiness, but I have yet to find that person. I'm not sure I'd want to.

When we are filled with that hunger—the sense of loss, or something missing, or injustice in our past—there is a companion piece to that awareness. We have some idea what we would like to have happen. Once you know, you can 'imagine what you desire, you will what you imagine, and at last, you create what you will.' Creativity is an expression of self-awareness. You only can be creatively expressive if you know what you want to communicate.

Ms Swift's thought that creativity should not end once happiness in life is achieved is a challenging one. We need darkness as well as happiness for contrast in our lives. Tennessee Williams wrote: If I got rid of my demons, I'd lose my angels.

Creativity demands one more thing from us (there's always one more thing, isn't there?)

Courage.

It takes courage to reach within, to explore or recall the experiences that shaped us. We may not understand them at first, which is why we return to them again and again, until we have taken everything from the experience that we can. It takes courage to reveal parts of ourselves that are so private, and express them to the world in a way that will be appreciated by those who read, see or hear our work, and know us a little better.

When I first read Taylor Swift's comment about continuing to be creative when we are finally happy, I thought she was referring to drawing inspiration from our joy. Certainly this is desirable, but the need for contrast remains. We appreciate a hearty banquet when we remember what it is like to be hungry. We appreciate our happiness when we recall that once we were sad or hurt.

Now, having worked through her thought while writing this piece, I realize that what she was saying was that she'd like to think we can still be creative when we are happy, because we have the courage to remember and not relive the less happy times.

> 'Creativity takes courage.'
> — Henri Matisse

Inspiration
12 April 2014

I am a writer.

First and foremost, it is my job to have thoughts and ideas, to explore them, and winnow the good from the bad. When I have had my thoughts and explored my ideas, when I have come to satisfactory conclusions about them, I commit them to print and make them available to whoever might be interested.

When life is rich in experience, when one lives in a stimulating environment, thoughts and ideas are like grapes—they come in bunches. But when one lives in a state of solitude, the harvest is not so rich—in fact, the vineyard may seem fallow.

This morning while I was taking a shower, I wondered what my next article should be. I've written a lot about communication and creativity, but I couldn't really decide what might be an interesting topic for you. I was actually considering who my favourite fictional spy from childhood was—it's was a toss-up between Napoleon Solo and Illya Kuryakin for men; Diana Rigg's Emma Peel was hands down the winner for the distaff side.

Then it happened—that little spark of incident that started it all.

I was just reaching for my towel when I heard a soft and pleasant sound, that of a solo bagpipe. I am descended of Scottish Lairds! (well, all right, some of my ancestors were from Scotland, *almost* the same thing) and in my view, the bagpipe is one of the three greatest musical instruments in the world. So naturally, whoever was playing had my attention.

At first I thought it might be the ring-tone on my mobile phone, but that wasn't it. Then, because the sound was soft, I thought it might be some other device in another room, but I realized I have no other devices. So it must be someone outside. I raced from one end of the apartment to the other, leaving little puddles in my wake, but I couldn't see the ground. I even called out, 'don't leave!'

My immediate inclination was to rush outdoors, but on reflection, I doubted my neighbours would understand or appreciate the immediacy of my enthusiastic need. I flung on my clothing and raced outside, but by the time I had reached the ground, the 'piper' had gone but left an intangible present for me.

Such a gift!

Suddenly, I had the idea for this article (do tell me how you liked it), and several thoughts about the book I'm writing. Although I haven't painted in many months, I felt a desire to get my easel and paints from storage and 'transcribe' some of the images this mysterious experience had given me (I probably won't; I'm a lousy artist). I even ironed my handkerchiefs in a tartan pattern (I simply reorganized the wrinkles).

These are some of the fruits of inspiration.

I'm not sure what's more exciting—having an entire set of ideas all at once, or watching a single moment turn into a vast landscape of possibility. Inspiration really is an important part of creativity—something outside yourself that prompts you to act. It is an instant that opens an entire vista of expression, and simultaneously fills you with an enthusiasm and energy for that expression.

In my own creative life, my greatest inspirations have been deceptively simple. A single poem was inspired by a phrase in a book; an entire story by a misunderstood sentence. I once composed a piece of music based on a theme of four notes. Simplicity is the richest inspirational element. Everything begins with ONE.

As to the pipe music, it *may* be that one of my pibroch-playing ancestors has pierced the veil of Time and Space, and has reached through the vasty ages to play me this 'wee aire'. (That seems rather unlikely—it would hardly be a *local* call.) It may be that some hiccup on my brain called forth this fantastic memory from the Well of Forgetfulness.

Perhaps I missed a call on my mobile after all.

It doesn't matter.

As to the piper, your name is a mystery to me, and I will probably never know you. But the world will know you. I'm making you a character in my book.

Carry on!

Commitment
18 April 2014

I've written about inspiration and creativity recently, so now let's talk about Commitment as an essential part of the creative process.

I haven't lived long enough to know how the concept of commitment has changed over the decades. I imagine (and hope) that in days of yore, commitment was an unequivocal promise to/for a specific result. To-day it seems that commitment comes with an addendum—I will commit to (whatever) *always assuming, of course, that it isn't inconvenient, too difficult, doesn't cost money or take too much time, require too much of me, and I don't find something else I'd rather do before the end is actually achieved.* I imagine we all know about *that* sort of commitment.

To prepare this article, I studied many quotations about Commitment; most of them referred to relationships, business models, and philosophies, as if there were no other focus. I was surprised to see little mention of commitment as a Promise, or an expression of Personal Integrity. I saw only one or two that referred to Artistic Expression.

I found, though, that all these quotations had one element in common: commitment embraces challenge and will not be swayed. That to which you are committed is desirable and challenging in equal measure. If you are committed to writing a book, painting a picture, or composing a symphony, you love the desirable and embrace the challenge because what is most important is that the book, the painting, or the symphony is given Life.

What interests me so much about commitment is that every commitment you make, whether it is to Some One or Some Thing, is also a commitment you make to yourself. If you succeed, you will find happiness. If you fail, even by default, you will find failure a bitter poison which influences future commitments.

To be Creative, there has to be a desire, an idea, a belief in one's self, and courage. Henri Matisse wrote that *creativity takes courage.* Commitment is an extension of courage. You have the courage to want something else, which in itself is a brave thing—to want change. You have the bravery to imagine something new and different, leaving the commonplace behind. You develop a plan of sorts that ultimately will lead to the realization of your Dream. In order for the dream to become real, you must be steadfast in your courage, make that promise to yourself, and see it through to the end.

Commitment isn't easy, and it is often simpler to say, 'this idea is too difficult, too impractical, too risky, for me to pursue.' How much do you want your dream to be real?

Some think that commitment limits freedom, but actually, it redefines and focuses the range of freedoms you have by removing irrelevant choices. For example, when you walk into a grocery, your freedom (your choice) is limited by what they have in stock. When you decide you want to make omelettes, your choices are refocused on what ingredients make omelettes. Within that redefined focus, you are free to choose myriad *combinations* of ingredients to create the Omelette of your Dreams. Not only that, there are a number of settings in which omelettes may be served, so you are free to choose *the* combination that creates *the* Omelette of your Dreams for *this* particular setting. All those choices are freedoms.

While enjoying these choices and pursuing creative ends, the object of your imagination and desire almost seems to take on a persona of its own. You adore that dream, and suddenly that dream is not as compliant as you'd like. In fact, it's being downright difficult and capricious. This dream is in its infancy, and like an infant, it does not always respond the way you want, or the way you think it should. You may have discovered, to your great alarm, the dream/infant can be improved, which means undoing a lot of work (which itself is a lot of work) and doing something different (even more work).

In the process, you grow as your dream grows, and you become stronger as your dream becomes more real.

Commitment is risky. Commitment is also love.

You love this idea, this dream, and your sole desire is for it to thrive! You could no more discard this dream in its infancy than you could discard a real infant. You care for it, work with it, nurture it, refine it, and the dream actually begins to work with you! It is quite possible to be inspired by your own successes. There is an element of Grace in commitment.

The Commitment of love is as much to yourself as it is to your creation. You deserve to have your dream become a reality—don't quit on it, and don't quit on you. If you believe in yourself and your idea, but don't follow through, you let yourself down. It's true, it may be difficult, at times it may seem hopeless, or pointless, but it *isn't*. No dream is not worth pursuing. As a person, as a creator, you deserve to accomplish and to succeed.

Nothing was ever achieved without commitment. Nothing worthwhile was ever accomplished without effort. Nothing satisfying was ever completed without love.

Don't settle for Nothing.

✢✢✢

You
20 April 2014

For the sake of brevity, to-day let's refer to writers, visual artists, musicians etc, as Performers. An essential consideration for every performer has to be the Audience—the reader, the listener, the patron of visual arts, etc. The Performer understands that a critical element of the creation is the Audience. What will the Audience take in, understand, appreciate? If I do *this*, what will they think, how will they react, and is it what I want?

The questions go on. You, the audience, make a vital contribution to what the Performers do—in fact, you make it possible for Performers to do what they do.

So let's talk about you, dear Reader.

Most probably, I don't know you as an individual, although I'd like to. While I may not know you individually, I do know something about you.

I know you've travelled a long time and a great distance to get here, to sit and read these words. I know the road between Birth and To-day has been difficult and yet surprising. Sometimes it's seemed easy or simple, and sometimes those appearances have been deceptive. It's been hard, it's been wearisome, and yet you've had the strength to get here, and that's pretty wonderful.

I know you've made choices that have seemed right at the time, and turned out to be utterly disastrous, leaving you to feel ugly, stupid, and foolish. You've felt flawed, which makes you like every other person on the Earth. I know you've also made choices that demonstrated wit, wisdom, insight, and were full of compassion and selflessness—choices that may have hurt you and required immense courage, but you saw them through despite everything, and someone else was blessed.

There are people you like or love who don't want you, and that's sad. If they were to let you in, they would find a real treasure in their midst. There are people who like and love you, who think you're the greatest thing to ever happen, and who profoundly treasure you. They may not be able to tell you—to express such deep feeling requires a degree of courage, and carries with it a profound sense of vulnerability, both of which can be overwhelming. Perhaps it's enough just to know they are there, somewhere.

I know there have been times you have felt alone in a crowd, and times when even your thoughts have made life seem crowded and invaded. There have been times when you've been sad or angry for what seems like far too long, and there have been times of happiness, even bliss, that seemed to end too soon. There has been sorrow and loss, and also joy and triumph. It's been problematic to find a balance between these extremes, and yet, here you are.

They say 'you have to take the bad with the good' (I'd like to find the person who first said it and punch him on the nose.) Things have happened in your life that were just plain *wrong*. Things that left you weeping long after you ran out of tears. Instances of betrayal, brutality, cruelty, and acts without compassion. I am sorrier than I can say that those things happened to you. I hope you won't fall back on that adage 'what doesn't kill me makes me stronger.' In my experience, people who can't deal with those brutalities say that to hide the hurt they still feel, and to pretend 'it's all good.' There is no interpretation of evil that justifies or excuses it.

I'd venture a guess, though, that because of those evil events, you reached out to others and touched their lives in ways you don't recognize and they will never forget. You'll do your very best not to allow those events to be repeated, and to make a better world—at least, your piece of the world. That's beautiful.

Yes, I know these things about you. You are a paradox–flawed perfection. So, you are perfect to be part of my audience. You're a person I want to reach out to. I rarely find out what you think, but perhaps it's enough just to know that you're there.

In the end, it comes to this:

I need you.

†·†·†

The Author as Created by His Characters
25 April 2014

There is a profound, almost mystical, relationship between an author and his characters, a Creator and his/her Creations. I don't know if this is a common experience among authors, but in creating the characters in the writing exercises I've done, my characters sometimes teach me something about being a human being that I didn't realize. They fill in the lacunae of my own human experience, and surprise me with their responses.

Some years ago I wrote a dialogue between a patient and his psychiatrist. The patient described a long series of traumas, and I, as the author, was very involved in setting down his history as poignantly as possible. When the patient-character had finished, I was very surprised that the psychiatrist responded, 'My dear fellow, that's simply *awful*! Where does that leave you now?' It had not occurred to me to ask that question. It's very true that sometimes we become so involved in our past that we don't recognize what it means for our present.

More recently, one chapter in my eBook 'Behind These Red Doors: Stories a Cathedral Could Tell' involved the confession of a young woman who had had a miscarriage. She had not wanted another child (she'd already had two) and felt that she had somehow killed the unborn child with her resentment. In the course of that confession, her confessor talked about her husband and his reaction to the miscarriage. In my experience as a counsellor, I've touched on this situation once or twice, but it never occurred to me that the husband might feel guilty because he believed his wife had lost the baby due to his own (physical) inadequacies. It took my character to teach me that (and it is not an uncommon reaction in men in this situation).

In the same eBook, I wrote of a WWI veteran who had become an alcoholic. One stormy afternoon he stumbled into the Cathedral and had an intensely inebriated conversation with the Virgin Mary. He was so drunk that he vomited on the Cathedral floor, and felt deeply ashamed. He cleaned up the sick, feeling humiliated, and at the same time, ennobled because he was taking responsibility for a situation he'd created, something he had not done in a long time. I would never have imagined such a counterbalance of emotions—my character taught me that.

In the book I'm writing currently, my protagonist walks away from an unwelcomed sexual advance by a voluptuous and uninhibited young woman. He does this because he recognises that the pleasures of the moment are not worth the complications and difficulties that will almost certainly follow. At the same time, he feels emasculated because a 'real man' would take advantage of the circumstances, and damned be the consequences! I had no idea, but it makes sense to me.

Perhaps I'm the character, and they are my creators? (Think of Chuang Tzu: *Once upon a time, I, Chuang Tzu, dreamt I was a butterfly, fluttering hither and thither, to all intents and purposes a butterfly. I was conscious only of my happiness as a butterfly, unaware that I was Tzu. Soon I awakened, and there I was, veritably myself again. Now I do not know whether I was then a man dreaming I was a butterfly, or whether I am now a butterfly, dreaming I am a man.*) You may understand my confusion.

A vital requisite of creativity is that you must shed your inhibitions in order for creativity to truly flow. That's much more easily said than done. Inhibitions are present for a reason—they protect us and keep us from doing things that threaten that which we most highly value within ourselves. They keep us from doing stupid things which usually entail us exposing ourselves to potential injuries and destruction (not always of the body, but also of the heart, and most certainly of the mind.)

If creativity is courage, it requires the shedding of those inhibitions—those barriers that are meant to protect the most sensitive and vulnerable parts of us. If we can do that, if we can lose ourselves in our creation, our creation will have Life.

Courage is hard come by. Smart people run out of a burning building; the fireman runs *into* the burning building, not because he is foolish, but because he values something more than himself. The enthusiasm, the purpose, the momentum of the instant is what carries him, and can carry us, to something new.

Creativity can be dangerous because it carries us beyond ourselves and our protections, causing us, in the rapture of the moment, to leave behind that to which we have clung out of self-preservation. When we cannot embrace that courage (and there is no criticism of the person who, in effect, does not wish to run *into* a burning building), the momentum of the moment can take us forward.

What is it we want to do? Paint a picture, or paint a really beautiful picture? Shall we write a story, or write a story that touches the hearts of others, however much it may intimidate us? As creative people we have a responsibility to our audiences. Many people live in the mundane. There is little beauty, little feeling, little exhilaration. They don't always want excitement or stimulation, but they want something more than they had. Our responsibility is to remind others that there is more than what they perceive as 'Life'. There is beauty, but it doesn't always present itself in the ways we've come to accept. There is excitement, and sometimes it leads us to consider life as something other than we've lived it, because our experiences, in the broad spectrum of things, are very narrow. There is more than THIS.

I do not know these things by myself. My characters taught me.

✦✦✦

The Flip Side of Creative Life
28 April 2014

Lately, I've read a lot about 'creativity'—the subject has presented me profound philosophical intrigue. Not only do I read daily quotations on creativity posted by the local art league (under the auspices of a talented silversmith), I read articles on several websites in which various aspects of creativity have been discussed.

There isn't a successful artist, poet, musician or etcetera who isn't creative. (To be a successful etcetera, you'd *have* to be creative.) There are plenty of people who are technically competent—I'm thinking of an organist I used to know who played well. She had the personality of an enraged Rottweiler and no sensitivity to nuances of expression, musical or otherwise. She could play the notes, and play them accurately, but that was the limit of her artistic expression. I would not call her a creative person, but one who was skilled in the methodical reproduction of other people's work.

People who can implement the ideas of others, but are hard pressed to come up with ideas of their own, are not to be spurned as artists. They would not be said to be creative, but they are talented and necessary; there are creative people who can't draw a straight line with a rule—they need as a companion the idea-less yet skilful implementer of dreams. There is a man on the East Coast who writes great musical compositions, but can't play an instrument or read music. Fortunately, he knows someone who can and they've developed a system, and his band is popular in the area in which he lives.

The more we explore creativity, the greater the possibility is that our understanding of creativity and how we define it may become narrower. For example, I'm very creative in the kitchen. A peach omelette with a Brillo Pad reduction (for consistency) is a very creative collation, but it doesn't seem to be a very effective or welcome one. I can't get anyone to even try one of my omelettes—some rubbish about not taking sweet and savoury together.

That raises a question: for something to be creative, must it achieve a particular kind or quality of result? Can we accept that creativity may have a negative outcome? How do these considerations shape our definition of creativity?

Another question is: who can be said to be creative? The recent material I've read seems to refer only to artists, writers, musicians (and the etceteras, of course). What about the rest?

Everyone is creative, but not always with a brush or a pen. People come up with creative solutions to problems all the time, but tend not to think of problem-solving or inventiveness as forms of creativity. (Some are very creative in problem *causing* as well!) During the winter, there was a serious problem with the gutter installations at the apartments where I am staying. They were alternately clogging and leaking, making huge cataracts of ice that, if they fell, could have easily injured or killed someone. The weather and severe cold prevented the owner from replacing the gutters, but the problem had to be addressed immediately. The owner and his son devised a system of chutes and funnels to prevent ice from building up anywhere it might fall on someone. It was a creative engineering solution, not artistic. (Then again, one man's mechanical contrivance is another man's abstract art, so their metal opus may qualify as the next great award-winning sculpture!)

Creativity is needed in every aspect of life, and always is comprised of the same basic elements that have been discussed here and elsewhere—self-confidence, non-standard/non-linear thinking, a desire for something better, courage, and commitment to a result.

There is a constant balancing of art and science in most things. We are inclined to think of art as visual, audible, edible, readable, and beautiful. We think of science as cold, clinical, chemical, mechanical, and physical. There is science in art—ask any painter who has tried to mix two paints to create a specific colour, and found that some of the pigments won't mix because they're chemically antagonistic. Barbershop quartet music is unique in that four singers produce five notes—the fifth note is the result of a sympathetic resonance in the harmonic. A rainbow is the result of the refraction and reflection of light through airborne water droplets.

Negotiation is an art—people are not all the same, and reaching an agreement with two people or more requires talent and sensitivity as well as psychological awareness and negotiating acumen. Camouflage is certainly as much art as science. Anyone who has looked through a telescope at the stars cannot fail to see the beauty of the sky. The Pleiades and Orion are beautiful constellations (but they're 'just stars'). Achieving difficult or unlikely outcomes in a situation require just as much self-confidence, thinking, desire, courage and commitment as painting a portrait or writing a poem.

Everyone is an artist in some way.

Please have an omelette.

Brainstorming
4 May 2014

Recently a gentleman mentioned that he'd been reading my articles about creativity, and wondered that I'd never mentioned 'brainstorming'. This, you may know, is a collaborative effort by a group of people to develop a new idea or solve a problem. I've always considered creativity to be an individual thing, so it hadn't occurred to me to mention it.

There are definite benefits to collective thinking. If you get together people who share a common focus and set aside personal considerations, this process can be highly productive. Keeping in mind there's a difference between creativity and manufacturing a piece of art, a group can help an individual come up with an *idea* for a poem, or develop a plot for a story, &c. In my recent writing efforts, talking with someone else sometimes has helped me unravel tangles or get around obstacles in my storylines.

Of course, it isn't limited to creativity of art. I learnt from my Marine friends in my 'smoky throng of smoking men' days that in the military, brainstorming is frequent and uninhibited. A group of people, from the highest general to the lowliest grunt, go into a room, close the door, and start a discussion with a view to developing an idea or plan that will solve the problem. Rank doesn't matter; anyone can contribute an idea or comment on someone else's. It is understood that you're free to disagree with another participant, even an officer of higher rank, but without personal criticism or abuse. Once the idea is created and agreed upon, when that door opens, everyone is committed to the plan. (I wish we had had such an arrangement when I worked in Social Service!)

A terrific example of positive brainstorming was provided in the film 'Dances with Wolves'. During community meetings, a speaker would rise and say, 'I have heard what So-and-so has said, and his idea has merit. I like that it has the benefit of.... However, I think that....' or, '....and it has given me another idea.' No one was insulted, this was expected and accepted, and generally with good result. Ideas gave rise to ideas, which is the beauty of brainstorming.

For brainstorming to be effective, it must be done without ego, with an open mind, and a commitment to something greater/other than yourself. (The same is true of Creativity.) If you're trying to make yourself look good, or if you shoot down every suggestion that comes from a particular person because of personal dislike, you aren't committed to the process or its outcome. If you have made up your mind before you've even started the meeting, there is no point in having a brainstorming session.

Rest assured that everyone in the group knows who contributed what, and if your contributions have virtue, you will be valued and appreciated by all.

It's odd, isn't it? Creativity is so often about self-expression, going beyond the limits of the comfort zone and exploring new territory. In business, the aim of creativity usually is to benefit the company, or the client, and benefits to you are secondary. Both kinds of creativity lead to the development of something outside yourself.

And so often, the idea an individual has will be prompted by the input of the immediate community—fellow business people, fellow artists, members of your 'think tank'. Just as a community of artists will help a fledgling artist grow by believing in him/her, and providing opportunities like art fairs, choir competitions—as a result of which the fledgling *grows*, the brainstorming community helps develop the idea that one person, or one group, will implement and make succeed.

Brainstorming doesn't require a large group of people—two people can achieve great things by exchanging and debating ideas. One of my practices is to talk to myself, act out scenes from my books, or read my compositions aloud. This gives me a chance to evaluate the writing, be certain I haven't used the same word too many times in a paragraph, and experiment with approaches that make the point I want. This does not help me when I hit a snag in the storyline, or wonder if I need to introduce another character. If I were writing only for myself, I would understand what I meant by *this*, and I wouldn't be confused by having too many characters—I have the inside track, I know what I mean.

Because I write for others, I need the point of view and perspective of others, and there are a couple of people to whom I can present questions and test plot lines. My clarity can be your confusion, and I would have no way of knowing that without the observations of other people.

There have been groups for collaborative creativity which have become famous. JJR Tolkien, his son Christopher and CS Lewis (to name just few) were members of an Oxford-based group in the 1930s and 1940s called The Inklings. They met frequently, to read to each other from their manuscripts, and get feedback. Similarly, in the US, the Algonquin Round Table in the 1920s was a group of literary wits, actors, and critics who gathered for daily luncheon as a collaborative creativity group—Alexander Wolcott, Harpo Marx, and Dorothy Parker were a few of the better known members.

To paraphrase the Gospels: Where two or three are gathered together, there will be an idea or opinion which just might be useful.

'Alone we can do so little; together we can do so much'
— Helen Keller

⁑⁂⁑

Behind the Scenes
7 May 2014

I hope you'll excuse me, I'm a little giddy. Yesterday I posted my third eBook, 'The Inn of Souls', on Amazon, and spent a couple of hours on CreateSpace. Now all three of my eBooks are available in both paper and electronic formats. (Okay, the commercial is over.)

I've been here before—I was over the moon when I published my first eBook, 'Behind These Red Doors: Stories a Cathedral Could Tell'. I put up a notice on facetube and LinkedIn, and the 'likes' and 'hurrahs' started piling up within a couple of minutes. I was very happily patting myself on the head and saying, 'Good boy!' when it dawned on me, no one had had a chance to read the book yet! This was a sobering realization I'm glad came to me.

I was feeling similarly smug and self-important late last week after I decided 'The Inn of Souls' was ready to go—there was no more composing or editing to do, and all I really needed now was one final proofreading session, which I planned for a couple of days hence. (Oh boy, look at me, I'm an AUTHOR!)

Around 3 o'clock the next morning, I woke up with a start and said, 'You have to rewrite the first and second chapters—they're too detailed!' In the morning I looked at the first and second chapters again, and they *were* too detailed! I also discovered other ways to improve the writing. I found that spellcheck is not an author's friend. It's almost as bad as autocomplete on a mobile telephone. (They're their, there sew mien two yew.)

A friend who sometimes demonstrates remarkable precognitive abilities sent me this quotation by Tom Hanks yesterday morning, just before I submitted my book to Amazon: *There isn't any great mystery about me. What I do is glamorous and has an awful lot of white-hot attention placed on it. But the actual work requires the same discipline and passion as any job you love doing, be it as a very good pipe fitter or a highly creative artist.*

This put things in perspective for me. It is thrilling to be a writer, and the response of the reader is both uplifting and seductive. It's possible to succumb to the accolades and huzzahs and forget that the really important thing is the writing, telling an interesting and illuminating story, and doing a good job overall.

'The Inn of Souls' took a lot of effort. I was going to tell the story by way of a series of first-person journal entries. The story was to take place during the summer months, and I later realized that writing a journal entry for every day (for three months) would be arduous for me, and boring for you. So, I changed the presentation to a first-person narrative, enabling me to say, 'Several days later....' Going over the existing manuscript was time-consuming, but I finally made all the necessary changes.

I was almost finished when I thought of a good twist to the ending. Ah, but now, to tell the story I wanted, I couldn't write it in the first person (and if you want to know why, you have to buy the book!). So I rewrote the entire book in the third person. This improved the narrative, and it improved the writing. It gave even greater flexibility to the story-line and expressiveness of the prose. It gave a much better ending than I had originally planned.

It was a lot of work, but really, it was a lot of fun. This is what a writer does. This is part of the creative process, and as Mr Hanks says, the actual work requires the same discipline and *passion* as any job you love doing. If an author is really committed to an idea, change won't be a problem, it will be fun and exciting. What will work best? What will the reader enjoy most? What will make the best possible creation?

I offer this illustrative 'tale' as a continuation of the series about creativity and writing well. I'm the first to acknowledge I sometimes stand in my own light and do a bad job because I'm busy admiring myself. Good writing is the fruit of humility; bad writing is a source of humiliation.

And in closing, I would like to thank the Academy, my psychic friend with the infinite supply of quotations, my Subconscious....

Oh, uh, and you, dear reader!

☙❧

The Dance
14 May 2014

A form of art yet to be discussed in this series on art and creativity is Dance. It's one of the earliest forms of self-expression available to us as human beings—a happy child needs no one to show her how to dance happily around the room. Dance is almost its own language, and like a language can celebrate or lament, can embrace, tempt or defy.

Several years ago I was invited to attend the recital of a modern dance troupe—I knew one of the dancers, who asked my frank impression after the troupe's performance. I know nothing about choreography, but I thought the dancers might have trained on a neurology ward. Their dance movements were largely comprised of convulsive gyrations and spasmodic jerking. I didn't see any beauty in it (but others did). My host was very amused when I told him I could make no sense of what I'd seen, and he said 'Dance isn't something you understand; you have to let it happen to you.'

Very recently, I've enjoyed watching video clips of performances by a young woman in Lithuania, who is a *fabulous* dancer. When she performs, every part of her dances—her face, her hands and fingers, even her hair, and not just her legs and feet. Her dance style is modern, but I don't have to let it happen to me. Her motions are graceful, disciplined, free-flowing, and she seems to me to express profound *joie de vivre*. Watching her dance is an almost liberating experience.

There's a nine-year old girl I enjoy talking to, because she dances through her conversations. She too incorporates her face (very expressive eyebrows!), arms and hands, and represents opposing points of view by dancing in one direction for the pros, and in the other direction for the cons. Her limbs contribute gracefully to her expressions. When she talks, she is fully involved in her conversation, even to the point of cavorting. Recently, she gave a spirited cheerleader performance when we found out the weather the following day would be comfortably warmer. My own response was, 'Ah, nice!' I like her reaction better.

As I've been thinking about Dance, I've realized that people are not the only terpsichoreans in the Universe. I've been walking a dog for a busy friend—when the dog sees me, she does a 'Circus Dog Dance'—she gets on her hind legs and prances about in backwards circles because she's glad to see me. I wish the humans I knew were so expressive!

People can spend years learning specific styles of dance—Jazz, Ballet, Hip Hop—and more contemporarily, to do specific dance steps, but no one really needs to *learn* to dance. It's part of us already. The infant lies on his back listening to his parents' symphony recordings, flapping his arms in enjoyment. This evolves within a year or two to the 'I dig your tunes and who needs a beat?' jumping/prancing/bopping. At some point culture and civility demand this lead to the Cachucha, the Fandango and Bolero, the Waltz and the Ballet. Sometimes, it even leads to convulsive gyrations. Dancing can be joyous, dignified, undignified, and mournful. These are states of emotional being.

We also have the dance of clouds across the sky, the dances of trees and blades of grass in the breeze. There are currents in the oceans and rivers—water dancing with the whales and the fish. The sun and moon have their own dances as well, and the stars....

The dance can be so languid you hardly know it's taking place, but the stars *do* dance across the sky, their movements changing throughout the sidereal year. Autumn leaves whirl across the garden, dancing with the breeze; trees bend and sway during the storm, yielding to a force greater than they possess, yet maintaining their own virtue—they yield, but do not surrender, to the force of the wind. These are utterances of Life in their simplest form.

We dance at weddings, we dance at parties, we *go* dancing with friends and lovers. We even dance with our words, hinting, testing, and not speaking openly. There is a minuet of meaning in the words that we say, lying there below the surface. Only your real dance partner(s) will understand.

Of all the forms of expression, I think Dance is the most open, most honest form when the expression is natural and not contrived. It's such a celebration! It crosses language barriers, cultural chasms, religious divides, age, even gender and gender roles. The most beautiful dances I can imagine bring people together—young and old, parents and children, and lovers in their many configurations.

So, dance!

The God Who Only Knows Four Words

Every
Child
Has known God,
Not the God of names,
Not the God of don'ts,
Not the God who ever does

Anything weird,
But the God who only knows four words
And keeps repeating them, saying:
'Come dance with Me,'
Come
Dance

Hafiz

✦✦✦

Simplicity
3 June 2014

Creativity is more than just being different. Anybody can plan weird; that's easy. What's hard is to be as simple as Bach. Making the simple, awesomely simple, that's creativity.
Charles Mingus

When involved with the creative flow, there's always the temptation to really 'take it over the top'. Why not—after all, creativity is a celebration of a kind, and you're letting out something you've been bottling up for who knows how long? Many of the quotations we read about creativity talk about freeing oneself from societal and emotional constraints, casting aside personal inhibitions, touching the chaos within oneself and bringing the whole universe to order. I envision an explosion that resolves itself into something peaceful and orderly.

Creativity isn't just about bringing out the richness and beauty within, it's also about restraint, balance and perspective. A flute solo will not be four times lovelier because it's played four times louder. (Similarly, and to my regret, something cooked at 350F for one hour will not be four times tastier if you cook it at 1400F for fifteen minutes. Those who refuse to eat my peach-and-Brillo omelettes have told me so, mostly through their refusal to dine.)

Creativity is not a single-step activity. You can't just 'be creative' and it's done. There are always the inspiration, the idea, the desire, and the PLAN for making a thought a reality. These do not happen simultaneously. Just now, I'm having lots of ideas, but that doesn't mean I'm being creative. I'm looking for the most effective way to express my ideas, which means I must know what's going on in my head and heart, because these will colour and influence my idea. Even at this point, I'm not being creative. Once I know what I want to say, I can start choosing my words, and I am beginning to be creative. Eventually, I'll finish and I will have been creative. There is no defining moment.

For some plans to become realities, experimentation must be carried out—nothing really looks or sounds that wonderful the first try. I can't think of a single act of creativity that did not involve immense amounts of practice! practice! practice! or trial and error.

August Rodin wrote: *The more simple we are, the more complete we become.* Think of the last time you were creative—you started with an idea, but you had to keep paring it back as it became more complicated. The idea would become difficult to manage and develop without keeping it simple. Every painting, no matter how complex, was painted with simple lines, and it was the combination of simple lines that created complex imagery. The same is true for music—the most captivating pieces begin with a simple theme. When you were finished, and your magnum opus was there for all to see or hear, your creation had completed you—said just a bit more about the essential artist.

An element of creativity is restraint, which itself is challenging. Enthusiasm can get the better of us, and we tear ahead, embellishing and complicating was started out as something very simple. I have ruined any number of stories and poems in just this way, because I lost sight of a crucial element—simplicity. Many of the 'elegant' embellishments I added (which contributed to the failure of my efforts) were nothing more than clutter or impediment, and added nothing of value at all.

That said, perhaps there's an element of *timing*, and this is where the 'universal order' begins to emerge. Creating an image, you need the form of your figure before you can begin to give it colour and texture. To try to do so during the rough-draft phase would be frustrating and unsuccessful. Later, when the image is blocked out and other, key elements are in place— that's the time to begin to adorn. If you were building a house, you wouldn't dig and complete the basement and *then* move on to the upper floors.

Confucius said (he really did!): *Life is really simple, but we insist on making it complicated.* There's always the temptation to take something simple and make it just a little bit more something than it was originally. With restraint, good timing, and a bit discipline, our efforts to be creative can be fully realized through our keeping it simple.

Simplicity is the ultimate sophistication.
Leonardo da Vinci

⁙

Pernicious Branding
31 July 2014

Every month, I attend several 'networking' meetings at which people introduce themselves and give a 'spiel' of no more than ten seconds. Of course, they go overtime, but no one seems to mind. The 'spiels' all sound practiced, and usually end with a glib tag line. Something along the lines of Gerber's 'Babies are our business—our *only* business!' Dorothy L Sayers had a good tag line at the end of her mystery novel '*Murder Must Advertise*': **Advertise, or go under!**

What I find disturbing is that I am beginning to see these people less as *people* and more as *caricatures*. One fellow with a video recording company had a very memorable tag-line: *If it moves, we shoot it!* However, I never did get his name, and I doubt I could pick him out of a line up. I don't remember who is interested in what, which fellow likes the symphony, or which lady writes poetry in her spare time (things that are important to me). Next month, I'll attend this meeting again, seated at the dining table with breakfast-eating businesses. Somewhere in the crowd are the music lover and poet I would rather remember by can't identify. If we see each other at a different meeting, we'll say, 'the face is familiar—what's your tag line?'

Of course, what we're discussing here is *branding,* and I'm not enough of a businessman to appreciate the importance of this trend. I am far enough outside the commercial circle, and objective enough, to recognize that there are aspects of a 'brand presentation' that are necessary, but other aspects that seem ridiculous. I think of myself as a humanist, perhaps even a romantic. I want stories to have happy endings. I want people to be nice to each other, and for the sun to rise in the east, assuring us of good life. I want the way to be gentle and beautiful, the songs to be sweet (and while I'm at it, I'd like a puppy).

Instead, everything is 'fast-paced', with bullet presentations of skills and acumen that may have taken years to develop. As a society, it seems our attention cannot be held for more than a few seconds, and consequently vital information has to be packaged, streamlined, condensed, and fired off in hopes that the listener will remember.

I wonder what that demand for the most information in the least amount of time says about how much we value each other. What does it say about my sense of self-importance, and my regard for you?

I've noticed a trend toward branding in personal blogging as well. One of the social media sites to which I belong is full of examples of people branding themselves with esoteric titles, such as 'immortalist', 'part-time voluntary worker, fulltime thinker', or 'karmalogist.' Some come with tag lines filled with pseudo-profound philosophies such as 'enjoy life, there's plenty of time to be dead.' I don't know anything about these people, and based on the evidence provided, I may be better off. Somehow an honest and open description, even if it doesn't fit into a few words, would be more illuminating and engaging.

Branding is not going to disappear because I don't like it (or perhaps I just don't understand it). When business trends begin to bleed into *social* media, I think we're beginning to lose balance and perspective, or perhaps the word I want is 'scope'. Certainly no one is likely to be engaged by an introduction: I'm an arranger of flowers, a lover of bird-song, and my dreams fly about me like leaves on the wind. Leave me your carpets, I'll get 'em cleaner than clean!'

At the same time, I don't want to meet some sweet young creature at a dinner party who introduces herself as an 'epulation aficionada'. (Brand-speak for 'I enjoy good food.')

It's a question of balance.

When you meet potential clients or partners at a networking meeting, or some other business setting, how much of what you present is the business, and how much is the real you? Some potential clients won't care if you like the symphony, they only want to know that you can defrag their hard drive. On the other hand, some clients are concerned about having a person with whom they can work (and build a lasting work relationship). Which is appropriate, and how do you know? Is a networking or other business meeting the best venue for this sort of thing?

Branding hurts—ask any steer. Is your brand hurting you?

✣✣✣

Ring the Bell
16 June 2014

Many years ago, when I was young and handsome, I ran a residential facility on the US East Coast. (Now, much time has passed, and I am merely young.) Although a lot of very positive things happened in this place—a lot of growth and recovery—this facility was not always a tranquil habitation. It also could be home to lots of contention and resentment. Clients argued with each other about the smallest things, or didn't want to comply with their obligations. Attendants didn't like what they were being asked to do, or spent time with clients they liked better than their own. I asked a carpenter for something of specific dimensions, the contractor wanted to give me something of different specific dimensions and charge more. Our funding source often impressed us with new styles of aggravation, most often through one of the subcontractors. Dark storm clouds gathered on our horizons, and it sometimes became unbearable.

As the tension grew, and the general mood became ever more grim, there came a point at which I would think, 'Somewhere in the universe, someone needs to ring a bell, and all this friction and conflict will stop. We will all put away our disagreements, hostilities and strife, go for a beer, and spend a pleasant evening.'

It was an agreeable thought.

I've been looking around me, as have you, and I can't say we really like what we see, do we? People have become nuggets of concise, concentrated information—so much so that you never really know the *people.* There are people so demanding, and exacting in their desires, expectations and requirements, that no human being will ever satisfy them. Entertainment is often an assault to the senses and the sensibilities—who can relax? In my view, the greatest 'sins' are the most common—insincerity, indifference, negligence and neglect. They are rife. A rat race in which the prize goes not to the fastest but the nastiest rat.

I'm ready for that Bell.

I want us all to hear that Bell so we can gather in a field somewhere, and stand around in a circle. Young and old, rich and poor, ruler and the ruled, lovers and haters, the different and the same—all together in a circle. Then we can see we aren't so different, that our desires don't always clash.

Those who were injured are healed. Those who were offended will forgive, and those who did offend will sincerely repent. Strangers will embrace and become friends, and the contentious will develop mutual respect.

Compassion can grow there. We can learn those that hurt us had reasons we could never fathom. We can learn that the People are governed by the authority of the Ruler, but the Ruler is governed by the needs of the People. Will we see that sometimes desperation was masked as villainy, fear as hatred?

There will be music. Not a symphony with its complex melodies and harmonies, a hundred instruments each playing its own part. Not a rock band playing at eardrum-shredding volume, but something simple, something sweet. A child, perhaps, playing a pipe, weaving a simple tune we all can sing, and to which we all can dance.

And when that's done, we can go for a beer.

And spend a pleasant evening together.

✠✠✠

'Passionate' is the New Black
24 June 2014

In pursuit of actual understanding of my fellow human beings, I spend a lot of time looking at social networking, blogging, and self-promotion websites;

after considerable study, I have to say people seem to have lost the ability to speak for themselves.

What I mean by this is the overuse of particular words. We live in the era of 'totally'. Recently, while getting onto a train, a woman complained to a friend that she'd just been 'totally hit in the head', and I expected to see significant damage, possibly with body parts lying about. Perhaps it was the blow to the head (which seemed innocuous to me) that resulted in her burbling 'totally' needlessly.

I recall standing on the street when a young woman came around the corner, talking on her mobile telephone. From the moment I first heard her until she went out of earshot, a period of perhaps 10-15 seconds, she used the word 'like' **_twenty-seven_** times.

The inability of wait staff to form a complete sentence when bringing your meal is a real tooth-grinder for me. I hate having my plate of salt-baked squid slammed down in front of me with the one-word injunction to 'enjoy' blurted in haste. It is, however, common practice in gustatory emporia.

I've heard more than one British English speaker complain about British youths' use of the word 'brilliant'. 'How was that book?' 'Brilliant!' 'How is your sandwich?' 'Brilliant!' I believe in the US, people have their own form of 'brilliant', and that's simply *awesome*. Literally.

There is a new villain of communication now. While perusing the biographical pages of such websites as

About.me and WordPress, I've found that everyone is *passionate* about what they do. In some instances, that would see quite reasonable. The Oxford English Dictionary defines 'passion' as a 'strong and barely controllable emotion', or an 'intense desire or enthusiasm for something.' It seems reasonable to be 'passionate' about child welfare and domestic violence, for example, or about your sweetheart. In other instances, 'passion' has become the new linguistic 'black', following in the footsteps of 'like', 'totally', and 'awesome'. Oh, I almost forgot—'brilliant' too. It makes people sound fanatical in some instances, and brain-dead in others. The mental image 'being passionate about' conjures can be comical, to say the least.

Skipping for the moment the fellow whose listed interests are himself, himself, and himself, and looking elsewhere while someone else says he 'writes with passion', we have a photographer who is passionate about light and colour, another person who is passionate about travelling, a gal who is passionate about crafting, and a guy who is passionate about hiking and mountain climbing. I was very impressed with one woman's page until I read that she was 'passionate about leadership'. Are all these people really experiencing a barely controllable emotion over light and colour? An intense desire for Leadership? (Watch out for that one!) Really?

According to Oxforddictionaries.com, the word 'passion' comes from the Latin *pati,* meaning 'to suffer'. Contemporary passions seem to have drifted from their origins considerably, unless of course your *passion* is to make *me* suffer. (Were we married once?)

When we fall into these habitual speech patterns, we allow a social trend or fad to speak for us, and we become sheep. The overuse of a word or expression eventually leads to that word having no real meaning. It becomes a reflexive, uncaring response or description which, in time, we learn to ignore. (The origin of 'goodbye' was 'God be With You', and it was a sincere prayer. Now it's 'bye bye,' offered without meaning or sentiment, if at all.)

There are some things I'm genuinely passionate about; I don't expect anyone to be interested in the degree in which those subjects, things, or people arouse my interest and affection. I'm satisfied to say I like something, I'm interested in something, I enjoy something. In the parlance of the contemporary speaker, I'm passionate about speaking for myself and not following trends and pattern fads, or being a ventriloquist's mannequin for *them* (whoever *they* are).

English is a beautiful language, and for it to retain its beauty, we must retain its integrity. Let us think for ourselves, and speak our thoughts instead of mindless claptrap. Of course the language will evolve—otherwise we'd still go around singing, '*Bytuene Mershe ant Averil/When spray biginneth to spring, The lutel fowl hath hyr wil/On hyre lud to synge.*'

Which, come to think of it, is almost as sensible as, like, I dunno, something awesome like being, like, totally passionate about potato chips.

※※※

Is this what we want?
7 July 2014

I've been corresponding with a woman who has been in prison since the early 1990's. We had been remarking on how the things we'd associated with our childhoods, such as penmanship classes and schoolbooks, are no longer evident. Instead of schoolbooks, young students now have eBooks, and cursive writing is not taught in many schools. This of course is due to the massive advances in technology that have taken place over the years. Who needs to lug around 'War and Peace' when you can have it on your mobile or Kindle? No one needs to know how to *write* anymore—it's all done on computer.

She was lamenting that her prison in Texas (unlike prisons in other states), didn't allow even limited, supervised access to the Internet, and even things like Skype and Google Plus (which provide video communication) were banned. Inmates are allowed iPods and MP3 players, but no access to music banks on the internet. With services like Skype, families who live too far away to travel to the prison would still be able to visit 'in person' with the inmate. She said she looked forward to her release, in part to throw herself into the scrum of communications advances.

Later, I thought about that conversation, and wondered if perhaps she were really missing anything. It's probably been going on longer than I think, but I've noticed with the introduction of the answering machine that technology has made it possible, not only to communicate more easily with people, but to avoid other people with greater efficiency as well. Caller ID allows us to pick and choose whom we ignore. The mobile telephone is a wonderful invention, but it's primarily use seems to be for texting, not talking. The same is true of wireless devices; go to any Starbucks and see how many consumers are talking to the person in the next seat. It distresses me to go to my favourite restaurant and watch people ignoring each other because of these damned devices while at the same time disturbing other patrons.

On the train, I used to enjoy engaging other passengers in conversation, even if it were idle banter. I met a lot of very interesting people in the old days, and even dated a lady I'd met on the commuter line.

Now, riders are glued to their device of choice, and the only conversation one is likely to hear is the one the loudmouth four seats forward is holding on his telephone. In consequence, I know more than I want to about the affair woman behind me is having with another woman's husband, and I recently heard a man rattling off a string of numbers to someone, with the injunction to keep the information private. (For the latter, I should be grateful I suppose. It occasioned some conversation with a couple of other riders, one of whom wondered if he should be writing this down.

The other said he expected to hear the launch codes for the next NATO sea trials. Fun stuff!)

Technological advance allows for greater indiscretion.

People are emailing co-workers whose desks are a mere three feet away. When I was a kid, one parent or another would bellow up the stairs, 'Come to supper!' Now, it's a text message (not even a telephone call!) When you call a company, you can conduct your business without speaking to a living person—computers handle that. Unfortunately, they can't answer your questions, but what does that matter to the company?

I wonder if my friend in prison is missing much.

This advance in personal communication devices is a wonderful thing, enabling people to conduct business and maintain personal contact over great distances. It has its drawbacks too. I was talking on the telephone with someone in Hong Kong, but we had to abruptly terminate the call because the bus on which she was riding had reached her stop. (I thought she was at home!)

However, these advances give rise to people being more and more self-absorbed, more isolated, and less social. People are so busy focusing on these little machines that they miss the rich opportunities that are right in front of them. They perhaps should think of the effect they're having on the people around them. Isolating yourself isolates me too.

It isn't that the old ways are best, but that we shouldn't allow them to disappear. The time and effort it takes to sit down and write a letter says a lot to the recipient; the email is not so persuasive or thoughtful. An honest to goodness conversation can be more uplifting and healing than any number of text messages (spelt of course in 'textspeak'—u no wht I mean?) We should not allow ourselves to be seduced by convenience at the expense of our friendships and associations. What will it do to future generations? Is it likely to lead to a renaissance of self-discovery down the road? Who is it in prison?

If you know (sorry--if U no), dial 3.

┼┼┼

Integrity
12 July 2014

The Oxford Online Dictionary gives two definitions of 'Integrity': first, *the quality of being honest and having strong moral principles*; second, *the state of being whole and undivided.* It isn't very clear to me how important or valued either definition of integrity is in the modern day. It isn't uncommon for very honest people to succumb to the seduction of 'slick practice'; to mislead or distract someone without actually telling a lie. 'Have you ever disobeyed an order?' 'I follow orders, but my superiors and I have not always agreed.' Many people would be satisfied with that response, but the speaker actually avoided answering the question with intelligent noise.

The second definition of Integrity could refer to many things. The *integrity of your ship's hull* will be compromised by a hidden reef. There is the integrity of a group effort. There is also the integrity of a style. Some artists are very concerned with this—not only do they want to create a particular image or sound, they want to do it in a certain way, usually the *original* way. Part of the problem is that fewer people know 'how it was done'. Military invasions, civil wars, and natural disasters have lost us knowledge that had been accruing for hundreds or thousands of years. In the 1940s, for example, Mao's armies invaded many temples and monasteries, destroying not only scrolls of scripture, but books on medicine, martial arts, and philosophical teachings. Many works of art were destroyed. The Native Americans have sustained similar losses of cultural wisdom and art.

There is integrity of a group effort. We live in a time in which individuality is very important (and I grew up in a time when nonconformity was the rage—they even had a uniform!) These days, dissention within a group seems to be quite popular. We've become so individualistic that thinking as a group is very challenging.

My personal lament, which I know is shared by others, is the loss of integrity of language. As I've written before, of course language will evolve over time. New technology, new approaches to existing problems and conditions, will necessitate new vocabulary and word usages. I am unable to explain the need to substitute the distortion of one word, such as 'ask', for a perfectly good contemporary word like 'invitation'. The frequent overuse of words blunts their meaning.

Over time, the meaning of words changes through conversational usage. It can be very interesting to observe. Take, for example, the beginning of this collect, taken from the Book of Common Prayer (1662): **Prevent us, O Lord, in all our doings....** Some might think He's doing that all ready, but what it means here is 'go before us', 'precede us'. It may well be that in 'preventing us' (1662) He is also 'preventing us' (2014), but that's another matter.

Originally, the word **presently** meant, 'very soon'. 'I will answer your question presently, but first....' Currently, it's used to mean 'now'. I am presently sitting at my desk.

I was recently caught out making a linguistic error of my own. I referred to doing a project and then doing a **post mortem** when it was done, and the man with whom I was speaking said, 'Now *there's* a word people often misuse!' He was right, of course. **Post mortem** refers to an examination *after death*, as any CSI fan can tell you. What I should have said was, **post hoc**, meaning 'after the fact', or literally, 'after this'.

Can we say that these changes are the result of loss of linguistic integrity? Does integrity break down over time, or does it evolve? Presently I can't say, but I may find out presently. (Who could resist?)

So the next time you're in your place of worship, bow your head reverently and say, 'Prevent us presently, O Lord, from post mortems.'

I'm not sure I'd understand, but I think He will.

✦✦✦

Dress to Express
16 July 2014

I used to see a man strolling along the sidewalks of the business district. He was a very distinguished looking man who always wore a grey pinstriped three-piece suit, a carefully knotted tie, a white, starched, French-cuff shirt, and a bowler hat. He had balloon-rim spectacles and carried a rolled umbrella. I never heard him speak, so I don't actually know, but he seemed the stereotypic Londoner from The City. When people saw him, they were impressed, and regarded him respectfully. You knew that he was someone important, and someone to be taken seriously, just by the way he dressed. In the few years in which I frequently encountered him, no one ever thought otherwise.

I'm at a time in my life when I don't really know what's appropriate or suitable attire because I no longer work the 9-5 salt-mines. I'm very much a free agent and I'm beginning to occupy a professional world that is very flexible. I attend a variety of meetings throughout the month, and I try to dress appropriately for each meeting. I'm not entirely sure how to gauge 'appropriateness'. If I shave, when I arrive at the meeting, many of the other men are unshaven; if I wear a tie, I may be one of three or four who did—the other men have open necked collars or tee-shirts. And of course, if I don't shave, or don't wear a tie, the party I'm meeting will arrive dressed in a hand-tailored three-piece suit with silk necktie, shaven almost surgically close, and smelling of a wisp of something spicy, slightly sweet, and probably imported. I never seem to get it right.

Choice of attire is to some extent governed by the season of the year. There are several shops near where I stay, and I see the staff coming and going every day. I have a much different sense of them when they're wearing Oxford shirts and shoes than I do when they're wearing faded tee shirts and sandals. The attire at the moment is less formal because it's summer; in the winter, these people make a much different impression sartorially.

Some people dress a particular way as an occupational representation. The clergy have their round collars; police, fire, the military have their uniforms. When I was on the East Coast, I often visited large international companies, and the quality of attire was always most professional. Doubtless, after the bell rang and they all went home, they were probably in sweat pants and sneakers, but that would be a different environment. While some national store and restaurant chains have a 'uniform' of some description, many other shops do not, and it becomes difficult to tell the inmates from the visitors.

We not only dress to express ourselves, we dress (or should) to *address* our environments. It's unsuitable to show up to the opera in worn-out jeans and a ratty tee shirt unless you want people to think you're a complete clot. (It's unsuitable to change the oil in your car wearing a Saville Row suit, too! People will think you're a snob.) When I was a boy, men and boys wore coats and ties to church on Sunday; women and girls wore dresses, hats, and gloves. To-day, it's wonderful if they just show up.

Choice of attire expresses the wearer's regard for the place s/he's in. It would be insulting to show up to a funeral dressed like an Easter egg (but I know a fire captain who had to be dressed by his wife to prevent such things from happening.) Would you be well-received at the UN wearing a shirt that said, 'Make tea, not war!' Given a chance to meet someone you've admired for a long time, what impression would you like to make? Your choice of clothes is telling. People notice these things.

As I mentioned, some people dress to represent their vocations. The attire is sometimes symbolic and represents authority, and other times is merely practical. Others dress to represent the magnitude, dignity or gravity of their work. In many Commonwealth countries, attorneys in court (barristers) wear a robe and horse-hair wig, to demonstrate respect for the law and the majesty of the law (and scare the hell out of the witnesses.) To show up looking like Gidget wouldn't have the same impact, would it? Still other people dress to express their individuality, conformity, nonconformity, respect or lack of it, and their regard for themselves and others in the environments in which you meet them. I suppose people are dressing to express themselves, but it's too bad so many of them require an interpreter.

When I think of that man in the bowler hat, it is inconceivable to me that anyone would ever laugh at him. When I think of Fire Captain Easter Egg, it is inconceivable that anyone would take him seriously. I think of some of the costumes I see on the street—they could scarcely be considered 'street wear'—they do not seem to me to express the wearer's individuality so much as they do her/his rage or contempt for convention by way of flamboyance. People want to make a statement, and this is certainly a way to do it, but is it a statement others will understand? Is it the statement you mean? You should be careful what you say and how you say it.

In fact, there is only one group which seems to have nothing to say for themselves at all.

Nudists.

✢✢✢

The Nonspecific Approach
26 July 2014

In a business meeting recently, Peter and I discussed various approaches to effective presentation. He was very detailed in his examples of presentation, whereas I preferred something less precise. In this instance, he opted for saying what a wonderful job a vendor could do, whereas I was more comfortable with talking about what had been done, and the result of it.

In my view, the Detailed approach has several drawbacks.

- **It is restrictive for you as a provider; it may commit you to producing results that circumstances make impossible.**

'For one flat fee, I will load this new software onto your computer network and have it operational on the first day. You will be 100% satisfied with this software and the quality of my work. I will also provide technical support for the first year—all for the same flat fee.'

May I ask when you developed a taste for charity work? For one flat fee, you will attempt to load this new software onto your client's computer network and discover that none of the current software has been updated since it was first installed. That shoots the morning. You will run anti-virus and anti-malware scans, which also have not been done in at least four months, and have to remove loads of toxic junk. The system will have to repair itself. By the time the network is ready to receive your new upload, it will be late tomorrow. None of these extras have been covered in your presentation, but must be done before you can proceed. Through no fault of your own, you've failed to meet your deadline. Additionally, the client in this example is so challenged by computers in general that he will have you on speed-dial, and you won't have an uninterrupted meal until the end of your contract. For one flat fee.

It would be better to say, 'For an initial fee I will review and prepare your system as needed. When everything is in order, I will upload this new software. Barring delays, your new network will be operational tomorrow. I think you will be pleased with the result. The initial feed also includes X hours of technical support for the first year.'

In both cases, you've told the client what you will do, and what the client can expect, but in the Nonspecific approach, you've qualified your claims and left yourself room to adjust. 'Barring delays,' allows you to update all that other software and run those scans as part of the service before making the upload. It also shows foresight—you are expecting the unexpected. 'You will be pleased,' is softer than 'You'll be 100% satisfied' because you can't guarantee satisfaction. Some people are naturally ornery.

- **Details can create unrealistic, or at least inaccurate, expectations in the person with whom you are speaking;**

'My approach to solving this problem requires no more than three treatments, and you will feel better almost immediately. You will be cured!'

No two people are exactly alike, nor are two problems, no matter how similar. The slightest variable can affect the outcome significantly, but because you've committed yourself to specific results, you're in a bind. Person A does very well; Person B is unresponsive, and you may find that Person B is doing something that blocks the effect of your treatment. Here, details put the entire responsibility on **your** shoulders, and Persons A and B only have to sit back, let you do your work, and expect great results. If they don't get it, it's your fault. After all, they're paying you to do the work.

It would be more prudent, then, to be less exact in your claims. 'My approach to this problem generally requires only a few treatments, and some people notice relief very quickly. You will be part of your treatment team. When the initial crisis is over, we can review and determine whether further treatments, or other changes, would be beneficial.' (That is to say, 'if you're being treated for high blood pressure, and you put salt in everything you eat, all of which is fatty fried food, we can discuss a radical change in diet.')

- **The Detailed presentation can make a client feel he has limited options.**

'I'm the best web designer you'll ever meet. I can design a website for you that will guarantee you a minimum of 10,000 hits a month, with a 30% increase in your revenues in the first quarter as a result. I do this for all my clients and they are completely satisfied. You can't let this opportunity slip by you!'

I would never take this approach. 'I've designed websites for clients that have increased their viewership by 50% a month, and have resulted in substantial increases in revenues. I would be interested in doing this for your company; I already have some ideas.'

No one likes to be told what to do. People like to make their own decisions, but of course, they don't always recognize their options, or evaluate them accurately. While there are people who will say, 'How can I say no?', there are many others who reject an aggressive presentation. When you talk about what you've done for other clients, and suggest what you could provide to your potential client, you've said all you need to. The client will make the decision based on the information you've provided, and will **own** his decision because you led him in the direction, and then allowed him to find the solution himself.

- **Too detailed focus may impair the client's ability to be creative with the services you provide.**

The other drawback to being to detailed in your claims is that you may unintentionally introduce tunnel vision into your client's thinking. 'I can write blogs for your website. I can give you three super blogs a week, for $X! I'm a terrific blog-writer!' (Notice—blog, blog, blog.) If you've been very focused in your presentation, and remembering that people don't like being told what to do, you're apt to get the response, 'We don't want a blog. Thanks for your time!' A less focused approach would leave room in the client's thinking for him to realize that, 'we don't want a blog on our website, but we have been thinking about a regular in-house newsletter, and he could write that for us.'

- **It can land you in court.**

I'm not an attorney, and this shouldn't be construed as 'legal advice', but we've all seen reports in the media of frivolous law suits being filed. They are settled out of court, or decided in court by a jury, for ludicrously enormous amounts of money. With this in mind, there are people who threaten law suits over the slightest disappointments. So imagine that you tell a client, 'This is a very easy task; with my modifications, it will take you no more than one hour.' When the client **can't** accomplish that task in one hour, he can claim (in court) that you misled him.

It would be better for both of you if you were less detailed. 'This is a simple task. With my modifications, you **should** be able to do this **in very little time**.' Your promise, and the client's expectation are more flexible.

I would like to say something about the ethics involved here. A nonspecific presentation may sound like you're trying to hide something, or con your client into a specific choice. This is not at all the case. What you say in a nonspecific presentation is the truth in general terms—the difference between 'it rained a lot' and 'it rained four inches!' You aren't overloading your client with non-essential facts. If the client wants specific information, he'll ask. Everything you say is true, but not so specific that differences become exaggerated irregularities. You are allowing your (potential) client to use his imagination, to make his own decision rather than you forcing a choice on him, and even allowing him to think of other uses for your talents.

However, let us not be **too** nonspecific. Otherwise, you'll be looking for the stuff inside the thing at the place, and I doubt you'll ever find it.

✦✦✦

A New Family
25 July 2014

Ordinarily, I'm not a fan of groups. The experiences I'd had with them when I was younger were distasteful, to say the least, and distressing in the extreme.

When I first went to the East Coast to run a facility for physically disabled adults, admissions and evaluation decisions were supposed to be made by a team. However, the team was so ego-driven that decisions were often made by one individual (not always the same one) and then forced through, despite constituting violation of federal regulation, incurring enormous expense, or putting other people at risk. I was glad when the team was disbanded and I was allowed to do my job.

Then there was the community group that was little more than a busybody's charter, gratifying the intrusive need for some to mind everybody else's business. The influence and power the community association wielded was, in my view, frightening—at best, a hindrance, and on several occasions, an expression of the deep prejudices of the governing few; again, feeble egos seeking validation through the exploitation of 'because we can'.

I won't say that's changed, but owing to a recent event, I am open to a new point of view.

On Monday last, I attended a business expo being sponsored by three Chambers of Commerce, and I met some really interesting people, including the General Manager of a company that rents temporary offices. She had been in the Navy in the Gulf War, and we clicked very quickly. So quickly, in fact, I don't recall how or why some information about me came up. I found myself telling her about my experiences with former Marines (which I wrote about in my post entitled 'Send the Marines') who, like me, have been wrestling with PTSD for some time. They took me in and treated me like one of their own. I never have felt so much part of something, or so accepted, as I did with those Marines.

Until this week.

The General Manager told me to look her up on Facebook, 'friend' her, and she would introduce me to a small virtual group of which she is a member. All of the people in the group were former military. Now in civilian life, their military experience was still a vital component in their lives and their thinking. As part of my introduction to the group, she wrote: **While he is not a vet with PTSD, he is a fellow human being with PTSD who in the middle of a very hard battle was taken in by Marines and treated like one of their brothers.**

Within an hour of her making this introduction, I began receiving very warm messages of welcome from members of the group, and for the first time in several years, I was part of something. Despite my total military experience having been smoking cigars with former Marines, they have brought me in and accepted me. I was greeted with **Semper Fi**, and one fellow said, 'Vado Exercitus!' (Go Army!)

This may well be the best week of my personal 2014.

I've noticed a big difference between this group, **Our Military !**, and others of which I've been a member. In other groups, people seem to be looking for a reason not to accept others. This is a primal instinct—in the caveman days, if I did not recognize you as member of my clan, you were probably an enemy and therefore a threat.

I can only guess, but it seems to me that in **Our Military !**, it's already understood that everyone is different; they want to find points of commonality. They're accustomed to working closely with people from different parts of the country who may talk funny, eat strange food, and have unusual regional folklore—that doesn't matter. They want to know how they can best bond with you because everyone may depend on that bond at some point. We are not friends or comrades through our differences, but through our similarities. They often refer to themselves as 'family', and it's very evident in their communications and postings that they take this seriously.

I've learnt one more thing in the brief time I've been part of this family. There is an enormous difference between government and the military, and there is a huge difference between the military and its servicemen and women. Some of the members in the group are very outspoken and indignant about governmental policies and decisions, treatment by the military, and how veterans are treated by Support Services and the public, and not being a military man myself, I am awakened by the depth of their rage.

Although they don't like what the government is doing, although they are unhappy with the aftermath of military service, **I don't believe there's a single member who wouldn't drop what s/he is doing to go back and defend the whole mess all over again.**

Semper Fi, America.

The Two Sides of Freedom
3 August 2014

For a number of years, I've corresponded with women in prison—'hard-timers', I believe they're called, and it has been a very satisfying experience for me. To-day, I am very excited because one of 'my girls' is being released from prison after a fifteen-year incarceration. I believe she did not get a fair shake from the justice system, but she has never protested her conviction. She's a brilliant and spectacularly talented woman who seems to be able to do just about anything, and do it very well.

While I'm very excited that she's left the twilight existence of prison and returned to the World, I'm also a bit apprehensive because I've known a number of ex-offenders who have adjusted to their release from prison with varying degrees of difficulty. To have lived in such a structured, regimented and narrow environment for so long, and then suddenly to be in a comparatively unstructured and limitless world can be frightening. We are defined in part by our environment, a sudden change of environment can lead to upset and distress. Service men and women returning from deployment can attest to this, I'm sure. Anyone who has suddenly lost a job will agree.

Thinking about my friend, I began to wonder about the nature of Freedom. What is a freedom for you may be a liberty for me. (Interesting, isn't it, that a synonym of 'freedom' is 'liberty', yet we have the expression 'to take a liberty'—a presumptuous remark or action.) That suggests that there is such a thing as too much freedom, but another way to understand that is your freedom may encroach on mine. That's problematic.

So, my friend may be 'taking a liberty' by doing something that is perfectly fine for the rest of us. If you want to spend time with an old friend, you can; if you want to go out for a couple of beers, you can. However, most of her 'old friends' are women with whom she's done time, and to associate with convicted felons (old friends) would be a violation of the terms of her parole. To have a few beers—another parole violation. The definition of freedom seems flexible and quite subjective.

I can't imagine how infuriating it is for law enforcement to defend people's legal rights, including the rights of criminals not yet convicted of a crime. Many of us know the term 'technicality'—an un-dotted I or uncrossed T, resulting in setting a guilty defendant free because his/her rights must be protected.

Parents and teachers raise children to be smart and independent; they must accept that at some point, they have to let these children make their own decisions (which is to say, make their own mistakes) and not interfere. Some parents never learn that there are limits to their involvement—their freedom becomes restricted over time.

There have been instances in America's history in which fighting forces were reviled by the people they were defending, at home and abroad. Those people were able to do so because the military being reviled risked everything to preserve that freedom.

We look at other cultures and see that women and children are subjugated and ruled. In some cultures, the patriarch's word is law, and among my personal acquaintances, it has infuriated me to see potential quashed by the patriarch's greed and selfishness. However, within those cultures, those we think of as subjugated frequently feel that this is their role and the regulation of their lives is perfectly acceptable. It may actually provide them with a sense of security. They do not understand our objections—do we have the freedom to object, or judge, or are we taking liberties?

We talk about freedom of religion and freedom of expression. Just as there are those who are flamboyantly 'religious', there are those who are offensively atheistic—no matter how objectionable to us, it is the atheist's right to openly (dis)believe as s/he does. I heard about a group that wanted to erect a statue of Satan in Washington DC—freedom of religion and expression say that they could. (I also understand they were prevented from doing so, but I don't know what legal instrument allowed that.) There really is no issue I can think of in which the opposing point of view, no matter how disagreeable, can be prohibited, because we all are free.

So I think about the nature of freedom, and how it is subjective, relative, but all inclusive. I'm proud of people who face freedom's nature and still defend it, because what's free for me is free for you, but your thoughts on freedom may not be the same as mine.

I'm even prouder of the people who can embrace it.

The Gentle Art of Subtlety
5 August 2014

For some years, I've been convinced that I really need to master the gentle art of Subtlety. In my youth, I did not hesitate to say what I thought, even when I didn't bother to think, and to do so in very clear terms. This earned me more than a few 'haters', but improved my long-distance running.

Since the cluster bomb approach to keeping friends has had a low success rate, over the years I have tried to find softer, gentler ways of expressing myself. This includes the decision to say nothing at all, which is often the wisest choice. However, I know I can do better, and I've done some online research to find the way. I want people to hire me to write for them, but when it comes to marketing and self-promotion, I'm a prize lemon. I've been looking online for examples and role-models. After trawling websites like LinkedIn, Facebook, About.me, Google Plus and a couple of unnamed dating websites, I have reached an inescapable conclusion.

I have no need to worry. I could probably teach classes. I practically have a black belt in subtlety.

The present trend seems to be one of Extreme and Excess. Yes, I found the expected bland and uninteresting personal representations. 'I am a _____. Hire me.' 'I have a pulse, wanna go out?' However, I found a considerable body of self-promotion that was more apt to make your target person scream and run for cover. One coffee house posted photos of counter staff, smiling and offering 'a cuppa Joe' (probably nothing so simple). The smiles were unnatural and unsettling—they looked like advertisements for dental bleach, and one staff member had a crazed glint in one eye. Mr Hyde, I presume. It's a question of 'eat or be eaten'.

People on dating websites were equally unsettling. There was ample representation of the 'dental bleach' crowd in pictures, but for some reason (and this was particularly true of female applicants), the effort to appear alluring and desirable translated itself into a facial expression of utter hostility. Given the descriptions many of these individuals provided, ('You'll be hooked on me!' 'I'm gonna rock your world!') bachelorhood seems an attractive option. I like candle-lit dinners and long walks—I'm not up for an earthquake.

Businesses, and individual entrepreneurs in particular, were also brazen in tooting their own horns. The Entrepreneur seemed to favour superlatives ('we are the best, you will get the most, this is the most jaw-dropping') and exaggerated descriptives. 'Extraordinary' is a word that came up more than once—how can that be guaranteed? They were like light-switches—either on or off, with nothing in between. Other people, promoted themselves, (sometimes in the third person) with obscure job descriptions: 'producer for boundless space,' or 'karmologist'. These fantasy titles are self-defeating. In fact, they are likely to ensure *the absence of continuous, structured, and focused productive activity of a professional character resulting in repetitive remunerative gratification*—ie: you stay unemployed. I won't consider hiring you, or hanging with you, if I have no idea what it is you do.

These efforts are inelegant and have an undertone of aggression, even extremism. Can you think of any situation in which either is desirable? The natural smile has been replaced by the stark white picket fence of teeth; the lovely woman in a simple dress has been swapped out for a sultry (read: sullen) vixen with a décolletage that started yesterday and finished in Nebraska. She wants to visit cataclysmic upheavals on your poor, lonely head, and all you wanted was a quiet dinner and conversation. The entrepreneur who wants your business doesn't demonstrate how he'll do a good job and provide examples of his work; he promises 'prodigious, stupendous, monumental results' because s/he is 'the most expert in his/her field'. The claims themselves are incredible, and the results are highly unlikely. There is no subtlety in any of this.

One 'benefit' of being a smart mouth in my youth was that I learnt to discern the difference between those who were tough, and those who acted tough. (For 'tough', you can read a number of other adjectives.) The tough guy never swaggered—he didn't have to. The guy who acted tough rarely was able to deliver. The beautiful woman has always been beautiful naturally—all the adornment in the world will not make her more so. You know the expert by his work—he doesn't have to say much of anything at all. The braggart, on the other hand....

The really smart, the genuinely expert, the truly excellent people never waste time on boasting and bragging. They're dedicated to the actual work, and it is their success that 'sells' them.

So much for examples of subtlety.

Late last year, a friend introduced me to a model of self-promotion that has become the cornerstone of my own efforts. He worked for The Container Corporation of America (CCA) for many years, and they had the subtlest advertising scheme I've ever seen. I'm hazy on the specifics, but I know that CCA engaged individual artists throughout the US and South America to illustrate a history of great ideas. CCA took out full page advertisements in newspapers and published these illustrated great ideas, and the only bit of advertising they did was this: across the bottom of the page, they put their name, in small print. The collection eventually ended up in the Smithsonian. In researching some of the details for this article, I also discovered that in the late 1940's, CCA commissioned someone to design a world atlas, which was distributed for free to 150 colleges and universities throughout the country. Their only advertisement?

They put their name on the book.

Now, that's subtle.

Living with Ghosts
16 August 2014

During the last week, I've been struggling with memories rooted in a catastrophic event (a fire) that took place in 2011; troubles compounded by frightened people I had thought were my friends, and who did more harm than the fire ever could have. I term these people, who are in my life only as memories, as Ghosts.

As I've tried unsuccessfully to resist being dragged down this particular memory lane, there have been also a few old, familiar faces from that time—people who 'raged against the dying of the light' with me, through benevolent acts.

It seems to be the Way of many blog-writers to be the self-appointed arbiters and critics of society in general, and I've regrettably contributed my share of negativity. From our armchairs, we rail, wail, and assail just about anyone or anything, freely and without fear. You can't be sued for your opinions, which is pretty much all a blog is. It's pleasant, then, even rooting around 'among the Ghosts', to rediscover acts of kindness. Those memories blunt the edge of fearsome recollection.

While I was in hospital, the day of the fire those several years ago, a man appeared in my Emergency Room cubicle. He owned a used bookstore near where I lived, and I often went there to browse and carouse. When he heard about my catastrophic event, he called **all** the hospitals until he found me. He came to see me right away, and afterward, I visited his store almost daily.

The following year, he helped me leave the East Coast and begin my journey to American Siberia. His store became a haven of sorts.

As kind as he was, his assistant excelled him in good works. As soon as I was released from hospital, I went to the bookstore to thank the owner, and I mentioned that I was concerned about all the books that I'd probably lost. There was one in particular that I treasured, but the title of which escaped me (even without PTSD, I have a poor head for names). Based solely on the **description** of this book, the lady did some searching and within a day or two, had found for me the exact book I was missing, and put it in my hands. The following Christmas, she gave me 'The Complete Works of William Blake,' the first Christmas present I'd had in years.

I've mentioned previously the staff and patrons of a cigar lounge in the heart of that city, and particularly, the former Marines who recognized my plight and treated me like a brother. I learnt that it's okay to wrestle with returning to normalcy, especially since the alternative is much less pleasant. The whole bunch of them helped me simply by not treating me differently from others. There was the photography professor who was my first 'victim' in my attempts to hold a conversation, and the attorney who used to discuss points of criminal law with me. He took me to lunch at his club one time—that was a stellar event!

Just after the fire, I went to a church for help (they were 'my brand'), and had to explain to an intercom, while I stood on the windy, icy winter pavement, that

I had an emergency and needed to talk to someone. I was turned away because I didn't have an appointment. I went to a Roman Catholic church some blocks away, and met a fantastic priest who had been a Franciscan missionary in Papua New Guinea for almost four decades. During the next year or so, we met as often as I needed. He listened to me, and did not judge. It's fascinating that the most helpful thing a person can do for another is often also the most passive. I learnt a lot from him.

Near where I was staying, mere blocks from the bookstore I mentioned, was a Japanese/Korean restaurant where I ate several times weekly. I used to sit at the sushi bar and talk to the sushi chefs. The head sushi chef, who was also the owner, sometimes greeted me with 'You look hungry' and started feeding me sushi and sashimi immediately. His wife often brought me special dishes from the kitchen, 'for health' she would explain. I formed close friendships with some of the waitstaff as well. I have to say, I haven't had a decent **Ojingeo-bokkeum** since I left the East, and I miss their **ebi, ika,** and **otoro**!

Those were the Angels of Then and There.

I don't know if I'll ever be out of the clutches of my Ghosts; they seem to arise when I can tolerate them least. I'm happy to realize, though, there are others, Angels, that kept the Ghosts at bay then, and I encounter some of their Angelic kind even now.

(That's one in the eye for PTSD!)

✦✦✦

Am I My Brother's Keeper?
19 August 2014

Last week's news of the suicide of Robin Williams was an unpleasant shock to many people throughout the world. It was an unwelcomed reminder for the public that Mr Williams was a whole human being, and not merely the talented actor and versatile comedian we knew. We saw him on screen and stage, larger than life, and relied on him to take away our pain, never thinking he might have pain of his own.

Although the news itself was distressing, I was more dismayed by the reaction of the public. I trawled the comment sections of websites such as CNN.com, Facebook, LinkedIn, which revealed the responding public to be selfish, arrogant and insensitive. Several people wrote, 'I didn't know he was so unhappy', but none of them said how (or if) they actually knew Mr Williams. (It is important, however, to appear connected.) Other commentators were critical and judgemental, describing suicide as cowardly and selfish, and depression as weakness or self-indulgence. There was no compassion or attempt at understanding, perhaps because these are 'soft' feelings, (and it is important to appear tough).

Suicide is an irrevocable statement that the person could no longer endure the hell that life had become. I see it not as a cowardly or selfish act, but one of desperation. Depression is a serious medical condition, based not only on a person's perceptions and reactions, but body chemistry as well. People with chronic depression are no more weak or self-indulgent than a diabetic who takes daily doses of insulin because his pancreas is insufficient.

There was another category of response that made me very angry. 'All he had to do was talk to someone. *I would have told him....*'

Really?

This is a world that answers bad news with plastic, sterile phrases: 'I'm sorry for your loss,' or 'Our hearts go out to the family.' There is no compassion or sincerity in those stock phrases, so overused they are devoid of meaning, and which fall on hungry hearts starving for real human sentiment. When we try to tell someone of a difficulty we're having, assuming we can get someone to listen, we may well be told, 'Let's put this in perspective; this has happened to me as well.' You realize you're being told your feelings of distress are not valid, because it's happened to others. (With friends like that....). Insensitivity has devastating effects on a person's emotions.

If we find someone to talk to, we can only hope that person will actually listen to us instead of formulating a response before we've finished our first sentence. We hope not to be told, 'Let it go,' or 'all you have to do...', or 'just do....' If it were that simple, we would have done it already. (It's important to note that none of these responses include any investment of time or commitment from the person making them.) These solutions, so glibly offered, are bereft of sincerity, and the sense of desolation grows.

When we are in pain, we want care, compassion, validation and support; often we receive excuses, rationalizations, and dismissal. The deeper our sense of isolation, the more profoundly such responses hurt us. Some choose not to risk it, and it shouldn't be a risk at all.

I think when we hear of the unhappiness and pain of others, it makes us uncomfortable because responsibility on our part is implied. Is this person telling me his problem because he expects me to do something about it? This woman is very unhappy; what does she want (what is she trying to take away) from me? When we hear of someone's suicide, (people we actually know, not people we've heard of), a thought persists—what did I (not) do? Is this my fault?

As much as we are responsible for ourselves, we do have some responsibility for others as well. We really are our brothers' keepers. It doesn't require a lot—trying being pleasant and see how that positively affects another person's day. Don't make that stinging retort, as satisfying as it might feel, and see if that improves the situation. If another person seems out of control, walk away instead of forcing the issue and making matters worse. Listen with a closed mouth and open ears instead of the other way around. While trying to understand the problem, listen with discernment and understand the person as well. The person is speaking to you from his/her point of view; don't make the conversation about you.

As an alternative to telling people, 'What you need to do is...', say to them, 'Why don't you and I try this?'

Be part of the solution, or be quiet. Keep your word, or don't give it, but don't go halfway and change your mind. Be consistent. Offer the person the choice of being alone, but let that person make the choice, not you. Display the kind of environment a person would want to live in, not leave.

We want our talented and funny people to distract us from our woes and take away our pain. We want our friends to love us and comfort us in our desolation, to help us, understand us and support us in our times of need. We want them to be faithful, patient, loyal and 'as constant as the northern star'.

That's what they want from us too.

The Centre of the Universe
26 August 2014

A member of a group to which I belong recently posted what she hoped was not a silly question: why do people no longer love their country? She cited several instances in which this appeared to be the case. Hers is a valid question, and I think it extends beyond just love of country. The same could be asked about many things we have held dear.

I think one answer is that our values have changed over a short time; we have become the centre of our own individual universes. We no longer care about the fabric of a country, so long as we are all right. We have lost sight of what is outside ourselves, bigger and greater. There are many manifestations of this attitude—you don't have to look hard to find examples.

What do we find? *We do because we can. We have the freedom to do so. It is our right.* This is Freedom. However, Freedom does not stand alone. It is counterbalanced by RESPONSIBILITY. The freedom to speak your mind is wonderful, and should be exercised responsibly and with discretion. Is what you have to say beneficial; will it do harm for you to speak, or to remain silent? Is it purposelessly inflammatory, and will it have a needlessly destructive result? Is it simply abuse?

There are venues in which speaking openly for your own satisfaction is acceptable, but in public forums, when other can be influenced or affected, discretion and responsibility must play a part.

The people who publicly accuse and abuse the government's policies and (in)actions, for example, help undermine public confidence and trust at a time when it can be ill-afforded. We've seen this many times throughout history. This erosion may be due to vehemently expressed opinion based on incomplete fact. The greater the issue, the less likely it is the public have all the details. If you have a freedom to express your opinions, you also have an obligation to get it right.

Discretion is vital to Responsibility. There is no freedom without an accompanying obligation. Imagine: you have an opinion, or certain knowledge, or perhaps you have taken a decision to act. Your information is complete and correct. You have the right to speak, or to take the next step. *At your discretion*, is this the most beneficial thing to do? Is it for the greater good, or does it serve your interests alone?

Another example of 'because we can' thinking is the Corporate attitude toward employment. I have heard from multiple, independent sources that it is not uncommon practice for companies to dismiss new hires scant days before their probationary period is completed. This saves the company the cost of benefits, pension, vacation time, etc. It is legal for them to do this. It is their right.

It is irresponsible, and it is cruel.

Not only is it damaging to the newly hired/newly fired, but to the newly fired's family as well. A single self-serving decision hurts spouses and children, but it is company practice. Company practice also damages the Public (taxpayers) because state and federal unemployment funds, already overburdened, must renew benefits for returning claimants. This practice shifts the burden of support from the company to the public. Is 'a penny saved a penny earned?' Whose?

It is unlikely many people have avoided the damage done by 'because I can' thinking. Sometimes this is expressed obliquely: 'this is how it's done', which effectively absolves the actual 'doer' from responsibility (even though s/he is the one who took the decision to implement this step this way). 'This is how it's done' is often overkill and detrimental, and in many instances unnecessary, but it is someone's right to exploit.

In all these occurrences, 'those who can' serve only themselves. It might be the individual getting it off his chest without regard for the overall effect. It might be the company that is more concerned with profits than people. Individual agendas are the order of the day. The common good (which is to say, the good of ALL people), for which people have struggled and died, apparently has been forgotten.

We claim to be a compassionate society. People risk their lives to preserve, not just American, but all human rights, freedoms, and safety; people at home treat them ill because it is in our freedom to do so. We film ourselves when we dump buckets of ice on our heads for charity, and not when we behave in an abusive or cutthroat manner toward vulnerable others, because we can. We have that choice. When our own needs are ill-served, or our egos need stroking, when we are unhappy about the state of the world, we are critical and abusive about those whom we have elected or chosen to follow, so that we can seem heroic, tragic, or both. It may erode confidence in the government, or the church, or whatever else we treasure, but we got it off our chests.

Does this help the country, or the People? Can we love our Country, or God, or anything else when we are so concerned with ourselves?

Ask yourselves then:

- Because you can, *must* you?
- This is how it's done, but *must* it be done this way?
- You have the right, and what is your responsibility?
- *Whom do you serve?*

There is no Love without Freedom.
There is no Freedom without Responsibility.

⁌⁌⁌

Ring the Bell II
5 September 2014

For the past week, I have wanted to write an article about self-definition—how we see and understand who we are. I can define myself by my ethnic heritage, my spiritual association, my profession, my physical and mental profile, or I may choose something really *depressing*, like listing all the things that I can't do. It's a question of balancing all the elements that make up who and what a person is. I have had difficulty writing my article because of all the distractions provided by Social Media and The Media.

This month is Suicide Awareness Month, and if you are depressed or suicidal, it is not in your best interest to read the awareness heightening material provided—it will depress you further. You can crush your spirits even more by consuming the output of the news media as they describe horrendous acts by fellow humans, foreign and domestic. They will do so repeatedly to be sure you've had your fill. I joined some support websites from which I am now backing away. After reading about the lives of my fellow suffers, I feel worse than ever, and much of the 'support' is mere rhetoric. 'Hang in there' seems inadequate to me.

I've heard from avid consumers of news, many holding opinions about what has been done, and what *should* have been done. Some of them can't separate action from actor, or accept that the public *can't* have all the information. They seem critical and irrational to the point of abuse. A bishop of my acquaintance once described people who did *not* read the news as 'irresponsible'. I disagree. I have communicated with people who never watch the news or read a newspaper. I think they may be self-preservationists.

At the beginning of the summer I wrote an article entitled 'Ring the Bell', in which I described a vision I sometimes entertain. When things in life become so overwhelming, I think, 'Somewhere in the universe, someone needs to ring a bell, and all this friction and conflict will stop. We will all put away our disagreements, hostilities and strife, go for a beer, and spend a pleasant evening.'

Reading a lot of depressing psychological statistics and recommendations, I realize the sufferer is expected to take the *first step* (practical but not necessarily realistic)—to reach out, speak out, hopefully not *lash out*, and begin a process of peace and healing. I realize, as I accept this realization, we all need to ring our own bell. The *first step* is that person's 'ringing of the bell'.

It is a question of balance.

While I agree there is need for us to have knowledge of what's happening in the world, the bishop was wrong. People who do not devour information provided by the news media are not 'irresponsible'; more fairly, they have a sense of their own tolerances and limits. The Media has a responsibility they seldom satisfy. Inundating the public with one disaster or atrocity after another, and with such graphic intensity, without counterbalancing information about the positive things that are being done is *irresponsible*. Media contributions have a powerful effect on the mood of the public. Statistics about the daily suicide rate are staggering (and depressing); how are they helpful? It doesn't take a lot of narrative to establish in the public mind that suicide is not a good thing. Talk instead about what can be done, and about what *we* can do. Try to reach suicidal and depressed people with *sincere* messages of hope and support. Private individuals who use social media to post articles expressing their personal outrage and fear, do so with such ferocity and frequency that for the public, it's like being flogged rather than informed. Personal bias plays a significant role in these postings—the lack of balance has an effect on others. Rage unbalances us all.

This actually does tie in with 'self-definition', so I get to write my article after all.

There is a disability advocate, a wheelchair user, for whom disability constitutes her entire identity. She is a crashing bore and a social-event landmine because all she can talk about is disability. It is almost impossible to imagine that she has any other interest, or can play any other role in life than 'disabled victim'. There is no balance when all you are is one thing. To counter that, there are many people wrestling with physical and mental health issues—their own and others—who are active and productive in their professional communities, avidly creative, active volunteers, optimistic students—people with bright futures. They have chosen to strike a balance. They won't deny their age or physical limitations, or their history of depression or that they juggle the extremes of bi-polar disorders. They just won't let that be *solely* who they are. They balance their internal struggles with their real-world output, and choose to see themselves as positively as possible.

If we cannot rely on the Media and the private individuals who delight in informing and scaring us with overwhelming negativity, then we need to take steps to right the balance. We need to acknowledge that we can only do this for ourselves. There is strength in having a positive and well-adjusted self-definition. You know your abilities and your limits (sometimes the most power tool you have is recognizing what you *can't* do). None of us by ourselves can save the world, eradicate famine, cure dreadful diseases, or end poverty. It would be wonderful to make greed and hatred a thing of the past, but they are part of being human (normal desires and feelings exaggerated out of proportion).

To balance that knowledge of our limitations, we still *can* save ourselves and help those around us. We can work for equilibrium between the good and the bad in our own lives, and perhaps in time, the doomsayers will get the message. Those who commit atrocities—especially lethal ones—do so for world attention. What would happen if the public didn't give it to them?

Let's ring the bell, if only for ourselves. I will meet you where Love, Sensibility and Balance abide. I hope you can't pick me out—that would be great! It's one time I want to be lost in a crowd.

✟✟✟

HELP is not spelt H-U-R-T
12 September 2014

September is Suicide Awareness Month, and many groups and organizations have increased their public visibility in order to discuss this very serious subject. Suicide is a *result* of conditions like depression, post-traumatic stress disorder, domestic violence, lingering diseases, etc. The statistics are staggering; the impact is frightening. I believe we are quite aware, although I do not know that we are necessarily better informed. We've always known that suicide is a terrible thing, and I hope we understand by now it is an expression that life has become an unendurable, very lonely, hell.

I have paid special attention to websites that offer support to people who are struggling with conditions that might result in suicide. It is nice to see so many non-professionals so deeply concerned, involved, and full of a desire to help others. Their enthusiasm is admirable. Drawing from multiple sources, I have read their pearls of wisdom, savoured their sage advice, and I would like to offer a suggestion of my own:

Be quiet.

I write this in considerable frustration. How would you feel if you said to someone, 'I have been depressed all week', and they responded: 'I've been depressed all month--you think you have troubles?' How would you feel if, when telling someone about a serious problem, they start shovelling advice at you without really knowing what it is you're saying? How do you feel when you're looking for *real* comforting and support and you get, 'Hang in there!' 'Keep the Faith!' 'Don't Give Up!'

Your cry for help quickly has turned into 'misery one-upmanship'. Hoping to have a conversation about your problems or needs, suddenly you find yourself talking about *their* problems or needs. When someone tells you 'Hang in there', do you feel you've established a meaningful connexion with someone who genuinely cares, or has heard *and* listened to you? Does 'keep the faith' answer your most pressing need?

Here is a cliché to describe the benefit of clichés: they are as useful as a sieve in a sinking rowboat.

As odd as it sounds, sometimes people do not want a solution or an alternative way out, they want to be *heard*. They've reached out because they can't find the answers, or the comfort, within themselves. Isolation is a terrible thing, especially when you're hurting. Engaging in one-upmanship, answering before you've been asked, lumbering the sorrowful with adages and words of dubious wisdom, increase the feelings of isolation. The need to be *heard and acknowledged* can be greater than the need to be fixed, and there's nothing more frustrating than trying to get something off your chest when the other person only cares about resolving the issue—your *feelings* aren't important.

Reality and resolution are fine, they have their place, but they also have their appropriate moment. The 'tough love' approach to healing does not help. I read one website posting in which a person was advised, 'this is going to be tough, you have to dig in, it's going to hurt, you're going to want to give up....' In that event, I'd take the trouble over the cure.

It isn't that people don't mean well—that's the problem, they *do* mean well, and don't know the right things to do. Unless you actually know what you are doing, talking may be the very worst thing to do. It is vitally, critically, supremely important to remember— what you are doing **_literally_** is a matter of life and death.

It's very hard for many people to reach out. I've been reading submissions from a veteran who is (according to his posting) so tough bullets flee from him, and bombs cower before him. The problem is that his tough statements reveal wounded vulnerability; to this man, reaching out would be an act of weakness. I hope someday soon he learns that reaching out is an act of courage. It seems paradoxical, revealing 'weakness' takes strength, admitting to fear requires courage.

So what is a person to do? How can we *genuinely* help?

Open ears, open heart, open arms, close mouth. Remember the conversation is not about you. If you have a shared experience, phrase it in such a way that you're not saying you know what the other person is going through, but that you remember what *you* went through and how can you help? You are not in competition to see who has suffered more. Do not offer advice, just listen. When s/he is ready for advice, s/he will ask for it. To have reached this point in communication has taken great courage (possibly prompted by the deepest sense of desperation). Support and acknowledge that.

When the time comes to offer help, be part of the solution. 'We can do this,' as opposed to the more frequently used, 'you need to do this, you need to do that, you and you and you.' In that event, feelings of isolation **increase**. No one reaches out to be alone (and reaching out for the wrong result is worse than being alone.) In order for this to be beneficial, you must be committed and see it through to the end. There is no place for changing your mind and withdrawing. That is a betrayal of trust.

I believe we all want to be heard, understood, accepted, and validated. We do not want to be alone, or judged, or told what to do alone. There is value in knowing others share your view that your difficulty is serious. There is freedom in knowing that it is all right to be incapable of dealing with a particularly painful problem on your own. Some people are so badly damaged by circumstance and experience that they can't or won't believe this about themselves, but these are basic human needs.

Here's another paradox—to be truly alone, you need other people to avoid.

◈◈◈

A Child Shall Lead Them
18 September 2014

The mind is its own place, and in itself can make a heaven of hell, a hell of heaven. --John Milton

With the publicity and public service announcements about Suicide Awareness Month filling time and space these days, and other special interest groups claiming attention because their conditions sometimes result in suicide, September has been a rather dark month. The information provided is very important, and the conditions and their potential result very serious, but I'm beginning to feel overwhelmed by all the bad news. I thought it might be nice to talk about finding tendrils of joy that make life worth living. I believe it has a lot to do with attitude.

Many of us are involved in the lives of others, and learn about the difficulty in people's lives. Some personal turmoil is inescapable, some is not. We cannot help illnesses—our own or those of other people. We tolerate the extreme thoughts, expressions and behaviours of others, no matter how much they grate on our most tender feelings. It is rare that to meet someone who had a genuinely good day, or has something to look forward to that doesn't involve making or spending money.

More and more people are living as if they're trying to get Life *behind* them (which has suicidal overtones itself). They give the impression that nothing (and no one) is more important than what is on their personal dockets, and they *must get it done!* Their lives are a writhing mass of complexities and (dis)stress, and relief often costs $20 a bottle, or $300 an hour. They leave behind a trail of hurts, disappointments, broken promises and betrayed trusts. The better qualities of their natures are blunted or hidden because '*I have to do this.*'

The sad thing is that they behave as if they were very important, (although no more so than anyone else), and that even they do not believe it themselves. '*I have to get this.*'

Recently I fell under the sway of a teacher who has been showing me how things can be done with joy. She is a charming and captivating young lady, aged nine-almost-ten, who I collect from school and bring home every afternoon. As we walk, she keeps an eye out for birds and small animals, which she is thrilled to see. She enjoys dictating nonsense into the translation programme on my mobile phone, and then playing it back in Japanese, Greek or Russian. (Did you know the Japanese for 'nanny-nanny-nanny' is 'uba-uba-uba?)

Homework requires fuel, preferably something noisy. I help her with her school exercises as she crunches away. Our greatest fun involves her maths homework. Every day she has twenty-six mathematical problems to solve. We have our own version of the television game show. She must solve the first twelve problems on her own. This is the 'qualifying round' for which there are no prizes. At question thirteen, I adopt my smarmiest voice and say, 'For the solar-powered elephant scrubber, an assortment of Squishies, *and* the trip to Disneyworld, answer *this* question: What is $3 + N + 2 = 14$?' She knows what the best prizes should be, and has won more priceless jewellery than Royalty ever owned. This has worked very well, but I still have no idea what a Squishy is.

There are occasional 'conflicts', which we resolve in a dignified manner—we make faces at each other until one of us says something poignant, such as 'I can see up your nose!' We have a giggle and move on. Many great people have spoken against silliness and frivolity, especially in adulthood, but it seems to me they have forgotten how desperately important silliness and frivolity are. (This is perhaps the reason grandparents enjoy their grandchildren so much—now they have the freedom to be silly once again.)

John Milton wrote that the mind is a place in itself— our attitude will determine whether we are in Heaven or in Hell. I think we often find that true in young children—in the midst of a flood, a child will find a way to play. We look at children and say they have not yet learnt responsibility and discipline. Might it be that they have not yet forgotten the freedom of childhood, as we have?

We don't have to roll on the floor, say silly things, or talk to stuffed animals in funny voices. We can look within and find that dormant element so often expressed by artists, actors, and other people with overt creative talents. We might live longer, but even if we don't, we'll enjoy it more. We can retain many of the things important to us and still have fun with the natural wisdom of the inner child. It's a question of balancing discipline and indulgence. We cannot live without both, and in my experience, we treat people as gently or brutally as we treat ourselves.

While you are contemplating how you might apply this wisdom to your own life, feel free to look up my nose.

Bring a Squishy.

✥✥✥

Like Mom Use to Make?
30 January 2015

Did you know that beer has a history going back to the 5th Millennium BC?

Did you know that as far back as 18th Century BC there have been laws regulating beer? or that Ninkasi was Sumeria's patron goddess of brewing?

Did you know beer is brewed in almost *every* country, including Egypt (in Ancient Egypt, it was a dietary staple for rich and poor alike; now you drink Sakara!), Lebanon (Almaza), and Jordan (Petra Beer)? Japan produces Sapporo and Asahi, to name a few; China produces beers as well—best known is Tsing Tao, actually a German beer brewed in the port city of Tsing Tao, but it's considered a Chinese beer. Singha Beer comes from Thailand, and is quite popular. India has more than one popular brand. The Tibetans have a type of beer called *Tchang* which is very potent. There are heady African 'homebrews', and Native Americans formerly brewed a type of beer from maize (corn). Beer is a global beverage with a very long history!

For centuries, households and taverns brewed their own beer, and each recipe had its own individual characteristics. Recipes were varied by the amount and type of fruit, herbs and grains that were included, as well as brewing methods. A particular tavern could be well known in the area for the quality of its 'homebrew'. The better of these developed into business breweries. Who didn't like visiting the Duck and Swan, who made the best March beer and October ale? And who wanted to wait around until the Duck and Swan was 'at home' to its friends? Better get it from the brewery and take it home! Household brewing drew much less of a crowd,of course, but could more easily cater to individual taste.

By the late 19th century, the small breweries either went out of business or were absorbed by larger beer manufacturers. To-day, a number of these have place on the multinational 'stage'. Even so, beer production is surprisingly regional, unless you're talking about Schlitz, Coors, Miller, or some of the better known European and Asian beers. In the 1970's, Piels was a very popular beer in New England, but no one in the Midwest had ever heard of it, touting Hamms as a local alternative. With the growth of multinationals, the joys and individualities of the local product were diminished or lost.

Plato said, 'He is a wise man who invented beer.' (Anyone who can develop a basic recipe that has lasted since 5th Millennium BC must be wise! And well-preserved.) Benjamin Franklin once wrote, 'Beer is proof that God loves us and wants us to be happy.' (By the 7th Century, beer was being produced by European monasteries, further proof of God's benevolence and approval!)

This wonderful and unpretentious beverage, and its variants, such as ale and stout, is associated with many very popular foods—hamburgers, hot dogs, hoagies (also known as poor boys, submarines, and grinders if they're heated), barbecue chicken and ribs. We never hear of people getting together for a sombre beer—it is a celebrative libation, and a meeting ground of sorts for the many and varied. Many people remember President Obama's peace-making between a police officer and a Harvard professor in 2009—the officer and the professor met with the president at the White House and discussed their differences over a cold beer. Traditionally, many union disputes have been discussed and resolved over sandwiches and beer. Beer is the beverage of the 'common man' (and woman), or perhaps, the beverage of those qualities which are common in all people. It is a liquid version of 'common ground', and many a conundrum has been discussed and solved over a brew.

Although the Duck and Swan's homebrew is lost to history, or was outdone by someone else's mug of suds, the multinationals do not completely own the market for beer production. In the last few decades, as our readers know, microbreweries, craft-breweries and brewpubs have begun to re-emerge, each with its own unique recipe or set of recipes, for local consumption. Once again you can have the beer that made your neighbourhood famous; that brew which drew like-minded drinkers from as far away as across the river because it was so good. This is a great thing, and in time, you can once again enjoy beer 'just like Mother used to make' (or perhaps, the beer made by Mother!)

Of course, there's also a downside. If you've been accustomed to drinking Mother Reginald's Lager from the microbrewery in Chicopee, Massachusetts, and then you move to Arcosanti, Arizona, you're going to feel a bit homesick because in Arcosanti, they'll have never heard of Mother Reginald or her beer.

Still, there is a certain pleasure in exploration, isn't there?

✣✣✣

The Tangled Web
8 October 2014

I recall that as a child, going to the doctor was relatively simple. The doctor's principle piece of equipment was his stethoscope, followed by a reflex hammer, and of course, his massive arsenal of hypodermic syringes. He had a set fee for office visits, and I never knew what that was.

In contrast, I saw my physician before I left the East Coast a few years ago. He remarked that he had 'gone through medical school and residencies to become a data entry technician'. Everything was done on computer. He had a stethoscope too, but aside from that, there wasn't much resemblance between him and my paediatrician. My childhood doctor smiled and whacked me with his reflex hammer before giving me the latest injection; my adulthood physician smacked a keyboard and remarked, 'An autopsy would be more informative.' He didn't give injections—you had to go to a specialist. He had a set fee too, but with co-pays and insurance coverage, I never understood what it was.

I started considering how much everything has evolved, and, putting technology aside as a consideration, how easy it is to stray from your origins. I have lost count of the number of times I have started this article. I wanted to talk about focus and commitment to an idea, but each time I managed to go off on a tangent and produce something other than I wanted. It's comical (unless you're me.)

I began writing articles for publication because I wanted to discuss human interaction, communication, language fads, creativity, and share reminiscences in rare nostalgic moments. In the summer I was invited to join an online 'family', which was supposed to be supportive; initially the experience evoked thoughts of dedication and doing right even when it was disagreeable. The group, however, appeared to have forgotten its original purpose, and developed into a platform for rant and braggadocio, so I left. Other events elsewhere excited my interest, and I became a rather intense social commentator.

That was never what I wanted. I don't regret anything I've written, and I don't disagree with my points of view on those matters, but I do regret leaving behind my original intention—to write positively, not aggressively, and informatively.

There's a difference between an idea evolving (one link connecting to another), and going from idea to idea the way an ape swings from tree to tree (leaving behind one for the next). The human mind cannot be said to be orderly (which why *logic* is a discipline). Even the most methodical thinkers are subject to stray thoughts and curiosities. The best thinkers do not forget their original intention, and they have the discipline to stick with it. As an example, the Nobel Prize winning physicist Richard Feynman was also an artist, known by the pseudonym Ofey. He sold and exhibited his artwork, and he never sacrificed his interest or work in theoretical physics to do so.

In contrast to Dr Feynman's example, many of us become distracted by 'shiny objects' and forget what it is we're meant to be doing. Singular purpose becomes a tangled web of undisciplined ideas and desires. Small thoughts, and small mental wanderings, have major consequences. The introduction of the computer in the doctor's office, for example, was meant to give the doctor more time to spend with his patients, except that s/he spends too much time on this 'device of expedience'. Many homemaker devices were meant to be 'labour saving' and are more complicated and time-consuming to use than their 'primitive' ancestors. The original intention has been lost or forgotten.

The Tangled Web is not limited to creativity, or to science, but drapes itself over humanity in general. A bit of distraction is normal and welcome, the way you might take a quick walk around the block before resuming your labours. For a lot of us, the quick walk becomes an exploration of unknown territories from which we may not return.

The problem isn't a modern one. In the Psalms of David, the psalmist wrote: *I am like a sheep that is lost; seek your servant, for I do not forget your commandments.* (Psalm 119:176). The Tao Teh Ching refers in several places to *returning to the origin.*

So, whatever we do requires full attention and focus if we are to accomplish our purpose. Some like to hurry it along, and do more than one thing simultaneously. Several cultures have a version of the proverb: *If you chase two rabbits, you will not catch either one.* This is characteristic of people who mistake activity for achievement. They splash about, and in the end, accomplishing nothing, and by now may be so frustrated that they give up their original intention.

Perhaps it is better to do nothing until you really love it, then love it completely so you can do it well. Be faithful to your love.

Great thoughts, great accomplishments, great kindnesses need an anchor.

⁙

Where Angels Fear to Tread
17 October 2014

At the beginning of the week, I had the idea to post a humorous article about Columbus Day, both as an experiment and because I felt like being silly for a moment. The experiment, in terms of quality writing, didn't produce the result I'd hoped. I would like to discuss this experience as part of the ongoing series on Creativity.

I posted my ridiculous article, 'Interludium', to see what the public reaction would be to a change in style and presentation. Written in the 'factual but ridiculously presented' style, done so well by the writer Will Cuppy, and the concert comedienne Anna Russell, I offered some silly thoughts about Christopher Columbus, and included a possibly off-colour statement about his three girlfriends, Nina, Pinta, and Santa Maria (who may or may not have been a nun). I suggested his weakest subject in school had been geography, because he docked in the Bahamas, called the place San Salvador, then told Queen Isabella of Spain he'd discovered a new way to India.

Ridiculous, as I said.

I withdrew the article six hours after posting it. Only three or four people had read it, and no one had commented on it, which relieved my discomfort somewhat. I'm not uncomfortable writing nonsense—my book, 'Lives of the Ain'ts: Comedic biographies of Directors Errant' is full of nonsense, as I meant it to be. I was uncomfortable about 'Interludium' because I knew it wasn't well written, and the style in which I had written it was neither well developed nor original. The whole project had been done with little care for quality. It was an experiment with an unexpected result.

It told me something about myself as a person who is a writer—I take writing seriously, I have standards, limits, and integrity about my work. I can't just dash off an article or story, I have to take time. Although I have always known these things, the experiment emphasized qualities I might have begun to take for granted. For me, this was a reminder not to be complacent or arrogant about what I do.

Sometimes we do a thing so frequently or repetitively that we create on 'autopilot'. We go from 'creating' to 'mass-producing' our work. For some (and this has been often observed in entertainers), success is the beginning of failure because having succeeded, they need no longer make an effort. Flexibility and the willingness to try new approaches and new styles keep the creative spirit, and the creation, alive. Complacency kills it. Some popular writers lose their readership after a number of books because the stories have become formulaic—you know what's going to happen, and when. There are no surprises.

Experimentation is important if a creative person is to grow through his/her work. Not every experiment is 'successful'—some can be flat-out embarrassing—but each is rich in information. You may find that a particular style of writing, painting, or comedy, is generally popular and works for someone else, but it may not be right for you. Perhaps it simply isn't right at the moment. You may discover you haven't found a suitable way to present your new idea to a receptive public. You might even learn that although the style and presentation are right, you have the wrong audience.

None of this is to suggest you shouldn't try, or that you shouldn't set out with confidence.

Before committing time and resources to a new project, a metal smith or a painter spends considerable time making study sketches—maybe hundreds! The composer, the poet, the novelist, fills notebooks with new ideas and their many elaborations. Much of this work is often discarded as junk. The artist must be convinced the idea is sound, workable, appealing, and within reach. S/he can comfortably and confidently proceed when there has been a marriage of restraint and disinhibition, and a balance struck between daring and recklessness.

> *Fools rush in where angels fear to tread.*
> Alexander Pope (1709)

⁜

Routines and Rituals
31 October 2014

We're all familiar with routine. We go to the office, but before we begin work, part of our routine is to get coffee, and chat with a colleague about non-work items before we've even sat at our desks. Then once we arrive at the 'work station', we must visit a series of websites, do the crossword or Sudoku, and finally tend to business. Do you know anyone who doesn't have a 'pre-work' routine of some sort? Regardless of what your job or profession, there will always be some tedium, which we all like to avoid.

No one just goes into the office, sits down, and starts working. We have to acclimate ourselves to the current environment. There's always some routine preparation and organization. The trouble with routine is that we can do it thoughtlessly, and it has no real meaning for us, other than delaying the inevitable. These often are delay tactics, of course, but they might be put to use as preparatory rituals as well. It depends on the attitude with which you approach the task.

The Chinese philosopher Confucius wrote that whether a thing is bad or good depends on our regard for it, and the value we place on it. Any task can be mundane, or become significant, solely through our approach and regard.

Routine can become *ritual*, a modestly reverent approach to the undertaking that lies ahead. During the ritual, there are many changes. While the physical environment is ordered and rearranged, the mental environment undergoes changes as well. The period during which a ritual takes place is actually a time of transitioning mental states. Until you came in the door, you were a commuter, a pedestrian, in a hurry to be some place by a certain time. As the ritual proceeded, step by step, you moved away from the rushed commuter, and closer to fulfilling whatever responsibilities have been given to you. Attention is redirected, attentiveness is refined, and awareness of your imminent role expands.

It depends on how you choose to view it. I suggest that if your first moments are spent in your personal *ritual*, you might enjoy your work more.

Imagine an artist—a painter in oils—arriving at the studio. Perhaps she has driven, or taken public transportation, to the studio. She may feel a bit frazzled by the rush to get to the studio, and want a moment to settle in. She makes coffee, perhaps calls a friend on the telephone, and then puts on her painting smock. She sets out and arranges brushes, other tools, paints and solvents, and considers how she will use each, and in what order. Every gesture invests some meaning and significance in what she has before her.

With each movement and each thought, the satisfying moment of the first brush stroke draws closer. A sense of pleasant anticipation builds. She savours the textures of the various brushes and the aroma of the paints. She enjoys the way the paint flows from the brush to the canvas, how the bristles bend and respond to the slightest change in pressure from her hand. She values her control over her tools and her environment. Different strokes with different types of bristles will yield different results—an art in itself. What she is doing has meaning now—she isn't just setting out a bunch of brushes and a clutter of pigments.

In this ritual, she has transformed from 'commuter' to 'artist', and is better able to fulfil her role. The ritual has redirected her attention away from feeling flustered as a traveller, to feeling satisfied and challenged as an artist.

Athletes, actors, musicians, artists—all have their rituals of preparation. It might be stretching, vocalizing, running lines—they contribute to a smooth, enhanced performance. Without the ritual, the performance, whatever the type, will begin roughly, and will suffer.

The difference between these people and the follower of routine I mentioned at the beginning is that the artist, the musician, the teacher, the athlete all love what they do and express the love through the ritual, despite the tedious aspects. The office worker with the tedious job might love the paystub he receives at the end of the pay period, but not really love the job. Perhaps a better 'harvest' might be reaped with a different ritual (and a different attitude). Through ritual, he can develop if not an actual love for his job, at least an appreciation for what it entails.

Any ritual is an opportunity for transformation.
                                Starhawk (Miriam Simos)

❧❧❧

Power Without Strength
15 November 2014

Consider this question: what is the essential difference between personal strength and personal power?

It is the characteristic of strength to be natural. It comes from within, and it isn't the product of any outside agency. It builds on itself and has a foundation, a definable origin. It can't be removed (without serious catastrophic intervention). It regenerates and restores itself. It is not subject to the understanding and acceptance of other people. It is synonymous with ability. It knows its own limitations, which can be expanded by step-by-step advances. There are many kinds of strength—the strength of the body, strength of will, character, and conviction.

Power, on the other hand, is not natural. Power is often accompanied by, and confused with, authority. No one has power naturally—in the best scenarios, power is earned, developed through discrete experience. But usually, power and authority, are acquired. In order to be effective, power requires the acknowledgement and acceptances of others. 'You are in charge because we allow it,' whereas you are strong whether or not other people accept it or not. Unlike strength, which provides feedback telling you that you've reached your limit, power has no internal feedback capabilities, and it is only held in check by what the practitioner *and* the people allow. As we have seen in the last century, power can exceed even the approval of the masses, with catastrophic result.

Power is also a companion of Control. At the beginning of the year, I wrote about control and its abuse: *The abuse of control stems from distrust of others, lack of confidence in their abilities/integrity/character, and is a reaction to feelings of vulnerability. When one feels out of control, the inclination is to try and control everything else, often with destructive and even self-destructive results.*

The misuse and abuse of power often results from feeling *powerless* (out of control). Just as the person who has no control over himself tries to control others in order to establish a manageable emotional environment for himself, the person who feels powerless may exercise power and authority over others—simply because he can, and this is the only thing that gratifies immediate emotional needs. Power pre-empts or usurps strength, the way ambition or greed can overwhelm wisdom and discretion.

Counterintuitively, the more power one has, the more vulnerable one is. Martial artists learn this very early—the greater the power (say, for example, using a weapon) the more likely and the harder a fighter is to be attacked. Because power is only effective when displayed, it attracts attention.

This is not to say that power is necessarily evil. Power is like any other tool—its character is determined by how it is used. Power should augment strength, not supplant it. To utilize power without accompanying strength is like having a flame with no candle.

When we have grasped these dynamics, where does this leave us? We have the parallel example of ethics and morals. An ethical person knows it is wrong to steal, to cheat or lie (but does it anyway), and a moral person simply won't no matter what the temptations are. There is a morality to strength (in fact, a synonym for morality, *virtue,* also means strength), and there is an ethics of power. It need not be the Power of an official over a populace; it might be the power of one individual over another.

Strength does not come from physical capacity. It comes from an indomitable will.
                                                              Mahatma Gandhi

One Thing For Another
28 November 2014

From a lot of the reading and writing I have been doing lately, I have become acutely aware of how easy it is, and how frequent it is, to mistake one thing for another. My last article discussed the differences between personal strength and personal power. One of my favourite expressions, 'mistaking activity for achievement', is a paraphrase from something I heard a long time ago on an English programme, 'Yes, Minister'. It was intended as a joke, but it stayed with me because that is what many people do—mistake *activity* for *achievement*. There were many truths mixed in with the humour in that series, and its sequel 'Yes, Prime Minister'.

Just as people confuse *power* with *strength*, and *activity* for *achievement*, they confuse *sex* with *love*, *piety* with *sanctity*, *opinion* with *fact*, *appearance* with *substance*, and *ethics* for *morals*. They will rule others, rather than rule themselves. The first is generally superficial, the second comes from deep within.

The Gospels speak of doing good and giving alms in secret, yet many people 'give alms' to get their name on highly public lists, or are conspicuously generous to improve their public image (and get tax write-offs). Many books on Eastern philosophy discuss 'holding fast to the centre', which, applied here, means avoiding the superficial to reach the substantial. Anyone can make a kind gesture, and many do, but there is no heart in that gesture. In *genuine kindness*, there is mutual awareness of the giver giving of him/herself. Georges

Bernanos, author of *Diary of a Country Priest*, wrote: *When the Lord has drawn from me some word for the good of souls, I know, because of the pain of it.*

For many years I had a friend who lived alone, half-way across the country. We spoke on the telephone regularly, and in the last years of his life, daily. He rarely had visitors. At Thanksgiving and Christmas, his next-door neighbours delivered a holiday meal. They didn't *stay* and eat with him, they had *other* things to do, and during the rest of the year, saw him only if they bumped into him in the hall. He had little contact with his children until he had been hospitalized for many months, but they gathered around at his death. All these people made gestures, but there wasn't much evidence of commitment or devotion to my friend. I may be wrong; I only know what he told me, and how unhappy he was toward the end.

In recent months there have been numerous atrocities, foreign and domestic, which have enraged and frightened people. Social and news media reflect this fear, opinion is rife and venomous, but actual fact is conspicuous by its absence. The response is almost immediate, whereas facts appear slowly. I refer to no specific event—there are too many from which to choose—and in trying to describe this state, the only phrase that comes to mind is *ignorance becomes wisdom.* So often, uninformed knee-jerk reaction merely makes things worse.

If people do not give adequate consideration to what they're doing, or to the result, unpremeditated injuring will continue. There are many people who give to charity, donate time to one cause or another, and yet are blind to the pain and neglect they inflict on those near them. How many of us know people who are so busy with things that interest them—perhaps even helping them grow as individuals—that they don't see the desolation around them that their inattention causes? Sadly, we often miss that which lies immediately before us.

Some will say this focus is much too narrow, and they may be correct. However, it is a real problem that affects a large number of people, regardless of how small a percentage of the populace they constitute.

Confusing one thing with another is resolvable. It requires, first of all, that people **WAKE UP!** and give deliberate attention to their actions and reactions. The things we feel and believe should be reflected in our actions and choices; our actions and choices should not be superficial. (What concerns me is that people's actions and choices actually *may* reflect what they feel and believe.) Actions should have substance, not appearance. Strive for commitment, not convenience. Perhaps we will not do as much, but what we do will be richer, more effective, and more substantial.

I had a meeting with a man recently who would not allow the meeting to end until he felt he had done something good for me (in which he was quite successful). Only then would he feel the meeting had been worthwhile.

We are often moved by stories of people who risked or gave up something for the benefit of others. The Russian Grand Duchess Elizabeth Feodorovna gave up her riches and life of privilege to open a convent and minister to women and children. During World War Two, many people risked execution by helping Jews escape from Germany and Eastern Europe.

Is this something we honestly see ourselves doing in any way?

Can we try?

✠✠✠

A Balancing Act
9 December 2014

How empathetic can you be without sacrificing objectivity? How sympathetic can you be and still be helpful?

The Oxford Online Dictionary defines empathy as *the ability to understand and share the feelings of another.* I can empathize with your feelings when you are told someone you care about has a dreadful disease. I can understand what you are feeling, but I don't experience it myself in any great measure. I can't really put myself in your place because I have never received any similar news. This draws on an intellectual analysis of the experience.

Sympathy, according to the same source, is *feelings of pity and sorrow for someone else's misfortune.* I sympathize with your outrage at being insulted, and what was said to you makes me angry. It is one of the few times the phrase *I feel for you* is actually valid—it is something I can experience acutely and vividly. This draws profoundly on similar experience and emotional memory.

These two are not necessarily separate from one another, but opposites on the same continuum. One can be sympathetic and empathetic simultaneously, although not equally.

It is not uncommon for people to confuse empathy and sympathy, to think without feeling and feel without thinking. Daily media provides a cornucopia of examples of both. It also not uncommon for people who have shared your experience to protect themselves by empathizing instead of sympathizing, because the emotional memory may be too painful, or too far in the past to be really felt.

We can understand and imagine how it feels to go through a divorce, for example, without having been through a divorce ourselves. Although we may not be able to relate directly to the experience of divorce, we remember what it was like to have a relationship end unhappily. (Our sympathy is engaged.) We may not have had to deal with the legalities of separation, division of property, and custody of children and pets, but we have had similar experiences to help us understand how it must feel (our empathy is awakened). We may have some feelings about that. One is never 'purely' one or the other.

Helping someone through a crisis, whether you have experienced something similar or not, awakens both of these awarenesses. Both are important in terms of your being able to respond genuinely, supportively, and comfortingly. You can be very empathetic with little or no discernible sympathy, and seem so 'clinical' that while a problem may be addressed, a troubled human being goes unvalidated. People in need require validation/confirmation—what has happened is horrible and painful, what they're experiencing is not imagined, and they are not alone—there are people who understand.

On the other hand, it is little help to anyone if you are more upset about something than the other person is—too much sympathy. You cannot have someone else's experiences for them—if someone kicks you, should I be the one to limp?
(A word of caution. At no time should anyone ever be led to think that because other people have had the same experience, the individual's pain and upset aren't real, aren't valid and justified, or are less important than anyone else's. There may be six billion lives on the planet, but each life is individual and unique, despite apparent similarities.)

In order to be an effective listener, helper or comforter, a level of objectivity must be maintained. This is difficult because by our very nature, we are not objective at all. Everything we see and hear we first see and hear through our own eyes and ears, and conceptualize through our own experience, or lack thereof. Objectivity (which the Oxford Online Dictionary defines as *the quality of not [being] influenced by personal feelings or opinions in considering and representing facts*) entails discipline (training) and maturity. In some walks of life, it relies on empirical information—how tall, how wide, how heavy, etc.

Subjectivity, on the other hand, is *based on or influenced by personal feelings, tastes, or opinions.* No training or discipline is required, and the experience and wisdom that come with age may not temper it—at best, delay objectivity.

As an example, recently a woman posted a Facebook imagine that mocked the Crucifixion. I commented that I thought this was distasteful (subjective), and was told 'To each his own', what seemed to me to be a careless and inflammatory response. Objectively, she was quite correct—I effectually chose to be offended because of my values. The image itself met the standards for acceptable expression by Facebook's rules, as well as those of the Constitution. Subjectively, I was deeply offended, I thought she should have known better, I felt great disappointment in her, and hid the item from my page.

You can see how inseparable empathy and sympathy are, and it is clear how easily objectivity can be contaminated with personal opinion. Pure objectivity, without a touch of *both* empathy and sympathy, may cause as many difficulties as it solves. It calls for a sense of Balance, which the Oxford Online Dictionary defines as *an even distribution of (something) enabling someone or something to remain upright and steady.*

Whether subjective or objective, sympathetic or empathetic, Balance of these dichotomous qualities must be sustained by Humanity and compassion. Oddly, in keeping emotions in check and preventing them from too heavily influencing a decision, or not allowing cold logical analysis to rule us and leave someone in emotional suspension, we must rely on something that is erratic and illogical.

Heart.

I love paradox.

•┼••┼••┼•

The Class of 2014
29 December 2014

We now have reached, to the surprise of some of us, the end of 2014, and we prepare to 'graduate' into the New Year. It has been a difficult, even painful, year for many, and there are as many opinions as to *why* as there are people. Many will blame the economy, but in my view the economy is a reflection for something worse. The answer is simpler than the economy. It's the human heart.

The greatest injuries one person can commit against another stem from indifference, insincerity, and neglect. An imbalance of passions stirs indignation, but also fear and unrest. 2014 witnessed profound injuries that were the result of these qualities in others. Some applied no restraint in using, or neglecting, other people (usually people for whom speaking up was difficult and unlikely). Others exercised freedoms guaranteed by law that would have been better exorcised, given their effect. What was most profound to me personally was this: a single word not spoken was more devastating than an epithet spat out in anger.

For me, there were **positive** events in 2014 that I am eager to share. One man told me I could share confidences about *anything*, and never failed his commitment. Another man refused to allow a meeting between us to conclude until *he* was sure he had done something good for *me*. Three women from different parts of the world (all of them hundreds of miles away) gave me substantial support at considerable inconvenience to themselves because I needed help. One professional spent hours helping me with my final project of the year even though it netting him nothing, while another lent his expertise to promoting my work. A renowned musician I know only through social media contacted me with ideas and support to increase my public exposure. I received all of this from people who were sincere, caring and attentive.

Why?

The answer was given to me by my neighbour's ten-year-old daughter in one of the most moving revelations of 2014. Early in December, I attended her school choir's Christmas concert. My little friend sang a lovely solo. In the last measures of the final concert piece, with animation and great élan, she dropped to one knee with her arms flung open. While the audience applauded the children, the girl standing behind her leant down and lifted her to her feet. I asked about this later, and my ten-year-old friend looked at me with a quizzical expression. 'She lifted me up because she's my friend,' she said. 'It's what friends do.'

That's why.

2015

Contrast
6 January 2015

During the holiday season I spent my time taking in DVDs and mysteries stories. Often I was reminded of the function of contrast and need for balance; the greater the contrast in elements, the more interesting the story. Trouble ended only once some semblance of balance had been restored.

A reader has sometimes commented that my articles start very darkly, or contain a lot of negative information; this is both true and intentional. Contrast is necessary. The significance of some really superb events in a person's life is vastly diminished without the 'backstory'—understanding the contrasting events that make those events superb. No one would want to read a crime novel in which there was no crime or injustice, from which the accused (?) was rescued by clever detectives and wily barristers to resume living a life of light and sunshine which he never left. A dark element would be necessary, and the darker the element, the deeper the interest of the reader, the better the story, and the more wonderful the outcome.

Similarly, in previous discussions about mistaking one thing for another, although elements such as empathy and sympathy, or strength and power, were not sinister, they were contrasting elements on a continuum. There are many examples of this sort of contrast. Children preparing their catechisms learn that a sacrament is 'an *outward and visible* sign of an *inward and spiritual* grace'. Contrasts in lighting and colour make an image visible or not, rendering it blasé or dramatic. To shoot the arrow, you must draw back on the string. Contrast (as opposed to distinction) is necessary. The Taoist concept of Yin and Yang is as much about contrast as it is about balance of opposites. When Yin and Yang are balanced, there is harmony; when not, there is chaos.

People don't always like contrast—they prefer not to see, or be reminded of, the darker parts of life. They sometimes yield to the temptation of oversimplified or selective thinking. A contrast does not always speak about good and evil, and in real life, nothing is ever entirely one thing or another. We all have the capacity for goodness within us; we can show genuine compassion and experience real joy. We're also capable of profound cruelty and unspeakable rage—there is not one person in whom these do not exist deep down. What gives us our character is the contrast between 'yin' and 'yang', and not just between good and evil, but (im)maturity, (in)temperament, (lack of) discipline, and (the absence of) self-restraint.

Without these reminders, however, the lighter sides are not as significant. Without an awareness of contrast, balance is difficult to attain, and balance is very important. The survival of the seven-year-old girl, Sailor, in the Kentucky plane crash last Friday is especially exciting given that the rest of her family died in the crash and she came away with minor physical injuries. The significance of the miracle rests in the death of four and the salvation of one.

It is difficult to come to any reasonable and sound conclusion about anything when only half the facts are taken into account. Until we appreciate this—if not the contrast itself, then at least that it is present—we will not understand who or what is before us, nor can we give fair consideration. It is difficult to really appreciate the beauty of something without knowing what the absence of beauty is like. The one who has been hungriest enjoys the feast the most! A small achievement, in light of background events, may actually be a huge victory.

Light shines brightest in darkness.

✢✢✢

Faith
18 January 2015

It has been said the difference between belief and faith is that you *believe* you can go safely over a waterfall in a barrel, and *faith* is actually getting into the barrel and taking the plunge.

There are many things in which people have faith. People have faith in God, or the Church (not the same thing), the Universe, or Destiny, and that everything will work out for the best in the end. People have faith in Democracy, Country, or the Justice System, for the purpose of maintaining peace and justice. Still others have faith in doctors, medicines, Nature and Science. They have faith in institutions like friendship or marriage, and the innate goodness of human beings.

In my experiences providing crisis intervention, and having presided at many memorial services, the differences between belief and faith are sometimes very pronounced. People believe the overwhelming problem facing them will work out, but it doesn't stop them from being sick with worry. People believe the dearly departed is in a better place 'on another shore and in a Greater Light', but they find no comfort in that belief. They experience tremendous pain. Faith doesn't protect you from ugly reality, but it softens the blow because Faith leads to Hope, making it more possible to endure.

Faith is the active expression of Belief. In whatever one has faith, the person is actively invested in something over which they have little or no control, but in which they have trust. No one controls God, and outcomes are not guaranteed, but we persist. No one controls the Justice System—it is a force unto itself; sometimes an innocent person is found guilty, and guilty people go free on a technicality. We trust our parents, teachers, and leaders, and are surprised when they are not perfect. While expectation is a good and necessary part of faith, too much insistence on that expectation becomes an effort to control. We can only have faith and an expectation (or perhaps better, anticipation) of a result—and open ourselves to Surprise.

Belief can change with time. As William Blake wrote: *What is now proved was once only imagined.* The flying machines of Leonardo Da Vinci are now fact, perhaps beyond anything he ever imagined. The 19th Century surgeon Theodor Billroth opined that 'the surgeon who attempted to stitch a wound in the heart would lose the respect of his colleagues forever.' The heart was the Inner Sanctum, never to be surgically tamped with—to do so was stupidity. To-day, hearts are stitched, repaired, removed and replaced. Belief will change as the facts change, but faith is constant.

Faith is not only the active expression of belief—'taking the plunge'—but can be active despite improbability, or even impossibility. We have faith that Country will prevail, despite the chaos in democratic countries— chaos that exists not only because Democracy allows it, but chaos that eventually resolves itself. We have faith in human nature—Chinese philosophers have asked, 'If you do not trust Human Nature, with what will you trust your distrust?' Some have faith that God will work things out in our lives, despite overwhelming indications to the contrary, and it happens. We call those Miracles. We take medications we don't understand because we have faith in the doctor, or in science. We trust in something greater than ourselves.

However, we also have faith in ourselves, and this seems paradoxical. There is part of every individual that the person does not control nor know very well. No one can truly be said to be knowledgeable of *all* his/her potential. We surprise ourselves by taking steps we'd never considered, by doing things we'd never thought we could accomplish. We thought we lacked the wisdom, or the bravery needed, and we were wrong. There is something greater than our self-awareness—our subconscious awareness of self.

Belief is very concrete, and tends to be grounded in fact, though facts may change. Faith is much more profound and flexible; trust that extends its tendrils into what we cannot control, and may not understand. It is important to have faith, because life without faith is desolate, hopeless, and joyless. There can be no faith without belief, of course, and while beliefs can and do change, faith tends to remain constant.

Belief and Faith are often confused, another example of mistaking one thing with another. It is important, particularly in difficult times, to understand that Belief is the fuel, and Faith is the fire.

It is the fire that lights the way

☩☩☩

Are You Sitting Comfortably?
25 January 2015

When you post a comment to my website, I must approve the comment before it appears on my page. This last week I had an unusual set of experiences connected with the series of articles I posted in 2014. I'd like to tell you about it; are you sitting comfortably?

At the beginning of the week, I received a comment on my August 2014 article, 'Dress to Express.' The writer of the comment ('PatriciaKa') said she'd been very impressed with the article, and had forwarded it to a friend who was so impressed that he took her to breakfast to express his gratitude! Three days later, I received another comment from PatriciaKa which can only be described as venomous. Oddly, it was about the article, 'Dress to Express'. The following morning, I received yet another comment from Patricia, this time about a notice of one of my YouTube readings, identical to the 'I got invited to breakfast on the strength of your posting' comment she'd sent a few days before.

Whenever someone sends a comment to my page, I receive a private notification from the webmaster, which includes the email and IP addresses of the comment sender. I did some research and found that there are over forty screen names—all of them connected with forum spam—attributed to PatriciaKa's Gmail and IP addresses—she most certainly doesn't exist.

It is of course disappointing that the nice comments weren't real (and a relief that the venomous one was false!), but in a general way, this was only a minor annoyance. I don't see the point of such efforts—it only annoys, no one will get any money, honestly or dishonestly, from posting false comments. There *were* a couple of other complimentary comments on offer, but I deleted them also, since WordPress's spam filter thought they might be 'forum spam' too.

People are very free with their insincerity—they say what they don't mean, they make promises they won't keep, they lead others to false conclusions, they praise what they haven't even seen or read. Who, then, is to be believed? How can we know?

While I was laying out the framework for this article involving PatriciaKa, I received a telephone call from a man whose company is going to provide a service for me. We spoke for some time, exchanged a few pleasantries (I'm pleased to say I made him laugh more than once), and at the end of the conversation, he said, 'I hope everything works out for you, and I wish you the very best.'

Because I had PatriciaKa in mind at the time, I found it difficult to know whether he was mouthing the words, or actually meant them. I would like very much to believe he genuine in what he said—I find a sincere wish almost as enjoyable as a good hug, and as heartening.

It needs only one person to spoil it for the rest of us. Because of people like PatriciaKa, serious well-wishers may have a difficult time being believed.

At the beginning of this article, I asked if you were sitting comfortably.

Do I really care?

Forgiveness
6 February 2015

None of us is perfect. By way of being human, we are angelic and demonic, wise and foolish, in control and helpless, hopefully *not* in equal measure. Some people have very positive attributes, and others severe deficiencies—kindness and consideration simply aren't part of their personality. Some of the kindest and most considerate people I have known are in prison for murder; some of the vilest and cruellest are in positions of public or personal trust. Generosity can be a gift, or a millstone around your neck—this has happened often. Knowing this is helpful and healing. You cannot expect a loving kiss from a scorpion, and you will not be disappointed or hurt that you don't receive one.

Probably one of the most difficult things to do in life is to forgive. When you suggest someone forgive another person, or forgive him/herself, a frequent reaction is discomfort. Perhaps it is because forgiveness is equated with weakness, the soppy sort of thing best left to mothers and priests. Certainly, popular films, television programmes, and fiction stories glorify vendetta and crippling revenge. 'An unjust action must be punished!' is the widespread view. To my knowledge, no one has ever made a popular film about forgiveness, perhaps because there are no murders, dismemberments, or cleverly cutting ways of saying, 'I forgive you.' We seem to like watching people being hurt.

Many religions, philosophies, and psychotherapy modalities stress the important of forgiveness, yet it still seems rather distasteful. I suspect that one reason is that our understanding of it may be backwards. How can we forgive those who have hurt us or wronged us, we ask, when to do so lets them off the hook? Why *should* they be forgiven?

Well, that's the backwards part. If I steal your purse, and you forgive me, I'm still a thief. If I strike you a blow and you forgive me, I'm still a brute, and the place where I hit you still throbs. Regardless of your forgiveness, I will have to answer to someone—God, the police, your friends—even my friends. Perhaps even myself.

The act of forgiveness is a *conscious* decision to let go of all that emotion. Don't forgive someone so that s/he will feel better, do it for yourself. The Buddha is quoted as having said, 'Holding on to anger is like grasping a hot coal with the intent of throwing it at someone else; you are the one who gets burned.' He is also supposed to have said (this quote has been attributed to other people as well) that holding on to anger is like drinking poison and waiting for the other person to die.

When the temptation arises to revisit old hurts, if you have made up your mind to forgive, you can say, 'I have already let this go.' The hurt feelings you have retained have become your responsibility, and you're under no obligation to keep them alive. I recall a conversation I had with someone who made some very caustic remarks about my disability. Rather than fight, I left. I bumped into her on the street a week later, and she apologized for her remarks. She seemed genuinely repentant, but I was still angry, and didn't respond. As she walked away, I realized I now bore the burden of responsibility for my anger. It was a valuable lesson.

Forgiving yourself is perhaps the hardest type of forgiveness to give. The bad decision we made some years ago still affects us, but it IS in the past. What else is there to do? Accept it and forgive yourself for not being perfect. Understand it, plumb your psyche for motives, learn from it, and move on. Why subject yourself to a lifetime of punishment (we are most often harshest with ourselves in this regard)?

Some people have found it valuable to ritualize forgiveness. Write down your grievance and all your hurt feelings. Pour yourself into this document, all your pain, your tears and all your resentment. Then burn it. It now belongs to the aether, not to you. You are free.

It should be understood that forgiving doesn't mean being foolish. If you slap me every time you visit my home, I can forgive you, but I'm damned if I'm going to keep inviting you!

✛✛✛

Secret Notes
13 February 2015

Recently I was sitting at a library table next to a very studious ten-year old girl, a friend of my neighbour's daughter. She was ploughing through her homework assignments as quickly as possible so she could join her friend on the library computer and play 'Minecraft'.

As we sat, there suddenly skidded to a halt between us a crumpled bit of 3x5 card—a secret note! I opened it and saw, written in a child's hand: **I LOVE YOU**. As I examined the note, I heard some youthful giggling and the rumble of sneakered feet rushing away to another room. 'I think this is meant for you,' I said, and handed the note to my scholarly companion. She read it, wrinkled her nose and pushed the note back at me. 'Boys are *so* annoying!' she said.

Things haven't changed much since I was a child. I never sent secret notes, but the excitement and horror of telling a girl how I felt was almost overpowering. The real excitement for me on S Valentine's day was crafting a beautiful card box from a shoe box, tinsel paper, lace, and foil hearts. The next day my beautiful box would be ruined by the other little kids shoving cards through the slot in the top and ripping the paper; it was supposed to be the cards that mattered but tainted the afternoon with sadness.

We were issued a list of fellow students, and to each we dutifully gave a card saying, 'Be My Valentine', even to the kids we abhorred. I didn't appreciate the irony then, as I do now, getting a Valentine card from the kid who gave me a bloody nose the week before. In theory, the more cards you received, the more popular you were. In practice, the more cards, the better list-followers the other kids were. We also had to give a card to the teacher. My second grade teacher,

Miss P, had the manner of a camel and the soul of a demon. Sure, Miss P, by all means, be mine.

It was, of course, insincere and provided us with a poor example of genuine expression of warm feeling. Better the hurled secret note of the timid suitor that landed on our library table. In Love, there is always a risk. Although he scurried away, at least the boy said what he understood to be his feelings, which is more than many adults do. Certainly his first effort surpasses the mass-produced 'Be My Valentine' cards.

Last year, someone told me she hadn't given me a card because she thought I didn't like S Valentine's Day. Not so. Valentine's Day is terrific, and should be celebrated every day! I am fully in favour of any and every opportunity to express love and affection. I am against commercialism, I am against insincerity, I am against 'going through the motions', and most particularly, I am against lying about feelings.

It can be easy to say 'I love you' when you don't mean it, and hard to say it when you do. I firmly believe in saying what you feel, meaning what you say, and behaving accordingly. I mean, let's be honest. Please.

I suppose I haven't changed much since I was a little boy. I'm still annoying, and I still feel excited and reticent about saying 'I love you.' I hope I wouldn't crumple up a secret note and throw it, although it's a lot more romantic than a mass-produced card that says 'Be Mine, (insert name here).' (Also to be considered is that although I'm far more mature than that little boy, his aim is much better.)

So, on S Valentine's Day I hope someone you love takes you by the hand, looks you in the eye, says 'I love you,' and means it. I hope you do the same as well.

May your S Valentine's Day be perfect!

(Now I'm going to crumple up this article, throw it at you and then run off. Be ready.)

⁘

The Golden Thread
1 March 2015

In all our lives, many threads run. We seem to like the idea of threads: they are continuous, and suggest permanence, longevity, and connectivity. People talk about blood lines as a way of linking the past to the present, establishing status of quality by showing from whom they are descended, and establishing hereditary rights. In fiction we follow a thread of clues from mystery to revelation. Even our lives are a continuous thread of moments, beginning with birth and never ending. Many are familiar with Shakespeare's expression in Macbeth: *Tomorrow, and tomorrow, and tomorrow, Creeps in this petty pace from day to day, To the last syllable of recorded time.*

These threads are metaphoric, of course, and not literal. The Classics tell about the Fates who hold the threads of our lives in their hands, deciding when a particular thread will be cut and a particular life ended. Lord Chancellor Sankey (1935) gave a famous speech about The Golden Thread: *Throughout the web of the English Criminal Law one golden thread is always to be seen that it is the duty of the prosecution to prove the prisoner's guilt....* Legal systems in every democracy depend on this 'golden thread'. Even the public attitude of 'innocent until accused' falls before it in a moral, well-balanced and well-ordered state.

The String Theory of Quantum Physics explains universal existence as all matter being made up of strings of 'quarks'—the absolutely smallest particle of energy in the universe. String Theory says the Universe is made up entirely of strings of energy! The universal fabric is woven from threads of quarks.

The important thing about threads is that they are constant. They may move or vibrate under different conditions, but they are always present, in time and place. Their impact may be significant or subtle. The fabric of your own life is woven from such threads. *Tomorrow, and tomorrow, and tomorrow* has led you from Birth to Now. All your travels, no matter how complex or erratic, have connected you from place to place. Your life has been made up of people (threads of relationships) that have helped define you, inspired you, given you a sense of purpose, constituting the fabric of your life. Your friends and family are certainly part of that fabric, and also, the stranger with the kind smile and gentle greeting that resuscitates your waning spirit in moments of darkness. People you know, and people you don't know, contribute to the fabric of your life. The gesture of a stranger may have greater significance than the gesture of a friend at certain points on that Thread. So, the thread may appear for only an instant, but is critical to your Life.

You yourself are a thread—your character, wisdom, spirit, and compassion—individual fibres that create *you*. Your role in Life is sometimes seemingly inconsequential, but has tremendous impact. Are you the person who listens to the songs and stories of a small child because no one else does? Are you the member of the public that makes it worthwhile for the pianist to perform, the author to write, or the painter to paint? You can't imagine the significance of such slight gestures, or the depth of appreciation that the person feels.

At other times, your participation is of greatest consequence. You are a parent, a teacher, a lover, a friend, a listener. You, as a thread, are a vital part of the fabric of the existence and happiness of others. Many people, at the time of someone's death, have been consoled with the realization that their participation in the Departed's lifetime gave it a fine quality.

Because the Universal fabric is made from *threads*, and because every thread has moments of subtlety as well as importance, every thread—every person—is vital to the continuity of Creation. Just as literal threads can create masterful, quilted works of art, the quilting of individuals can encourage and even create a tapestry of life that is amazing. This is something we can treasure, and realize our role in the lives of others.

No one is not necessary.

Heroism
17 March 2015

In recent weeks, I've been trying to understand the concept of heroism. I've watched a number of popular films, and found the heroes to be egotistical, smug and smarmy, imbued with some sort of special ability, and often not particularly likeable. They usually dress in revealing costumes that in actual life would be considered inappropriate outside a strip club. They are brash, noble to the point of being insufferable, and are inclined to suck up so much attention that everyone else disappears. They are no one you would want at your dinner table. As Ralph Waldo Emerson wrote: *Every hero becomes a bore at last.* At least in this regard.

I have studied the prime-time television and literary heroes also. These are men and women who can't leap over tall buildings, but think faster than a speeding bullet. Not more powerful than a locomotive, they harness enormous intellectual and natural energies. Lacking special abilities like invisibility, telepathy or flight, they are brilliant in their fields, solve crimes or make incredible discoveries, and their only costumes may be a lab coat, or a badge and a gun. Unlike their cinematic grandiose counterparts, over time we discover they have backstories, generally revealing deficiencies, tragedies, crisis and conflict. This is to make them more seem more real.

I come away from episodes of CSI: Miami (sadly, now defunct) and NCIS thinking, 'Horatio Caine—what a terrific guy he is! I wouldn't mind *him* for a friend,' or 'Leroy Jethro Gibbs—fantastic! Strong, noble, humble, modest, and no nonsense! I wish he'd been with me in high school!'

The principle difference between the two types is that the second type is rather ordinary in his or her abilities, and is much more credible. If they have anything extra, it is something they have built from ordinary abilities and qualities. They have reached within and done great things.

Being a hero is a matter of degree. Some throw themselves on bombs to protect others, and no one doubts their heroism. Some give the last chop on the plate to their children, and no one recognizes their heroism. Some are celebrities because they're heroes, others are heroes because they are celebrities, and still others are heroes because they are unknown. Our teachers, historical figures, and even celebrities, can be heroes simply because we admire them, and although they may have done nothing particularly heroic.

I asked someone for his definition of what made someone a hero. His first thoughts were for police, firefighters, and the military. He was especially appreciative of those people who were committed to preserving the safety and security of his family, handling matters no one knew existed. He may have been speaking of spies, but that's classified.

I agree with him, and I have some thoughts of my own to add.

I think *you* are a hero—not in the 'leap over tall buildings' sense, but in the sense of having heroic qualities. Heroism is more often the result of a quality than an activity. How often do you give of yourself and look for no reward? Or more probably, give of yourself knowing you will receive no reward, but do it anyway? How often do you face challenges that are significant to you (if to no one else), and persevere despite the difficulty? How often do you not make that cutting remark, embrace inconvenience for the sake of another, or walk away to preserve the peace? You are a hero.

I think the person who deliberately gets out of bed and goes to a job he despises in order to support his family is a hero. He might say he has no choice, but he does—he could stay in bed and let the family starve. The person in a difficult situation and doesn't do anything is a hero because she isn't making it worse. When she knows what to do, and does it, she will still be a hero drawing on different heroic qualities. The person who makes promises and keeps them, even at his own expense, is a hero. I think anyone who does something selfless, even at his or her own expense, is a hero. The person who faces any fear, no matter how trifling or massive, is a hero. Heroism isn't just about doing for others, it's also about doing for yourself in trying circumstances, bringing out your real qualities and putting away masks and excuses.

Anyone who can be The Real Self is a hero.

Dumbledore: Gay or Loving?
25 March 2015

Many have read and enjoyed the *Harry Potter* book series. They were a delightful and uncomplicated means of escape from the burdens of our own lives, however great or small those burdens may have been, and allowed us to sojourn for a while a world in which the most onerous things could be managed with magic. These books were written by JK Rowling, whose personal success story suggests that a good bit of magic, or divine grace, was involved.

About ten years ago, she made a startling revelation: Dumbledore, the headmaster of Hogwarts School of Witchcraft And Wizardry, was gay. She said, 'It has certainly never been news to me that a brave and brilliant man could love other men.' The news was caught up by the **global media**: a *fictional* character was *gay!*

Big deal.

Well actually, it *is* a bit of a big deal. I don't know why the author would want us to think that Dumbledore was a pederast, but the implication is there. Rowling has quite correctly pointed out that her characters can be anything she wants them to be—this is the prerogative of the author. Perhaps she has forgotten that too much fact can obscure a story as well as too little. When creating characters, there are features that help an author know a character and portray him/her with greater scope, but aren't necessary for the public. If Dumbledore's sexuality *had* to be mentioned, then it should have played a visible role in the tales. The inclusion of this detail added nothing to the books and it was entirely unnecessary to mention, especially after the final book had been published (but it did increase post-publication interest in the books, a sly marketing ploy).

In the decade since, Rowling has been called upon to explain or defend that revelation again and again. I thought it unfortunate; one thing I enjoyed about the *Harry Potter* books was the *lack* of sexual complication. Many contemporary books and films have been marred by pointless scenes of fumbling in the bedroom and the details of whom and what a character likes to engage on a physical level. They add nothing to the tale, they only satisfied public prurience. How many classics in literature and film succeeded without semi-pornographic interludes?

Rowling may have made a positive impression by responding to a fan who couldn't see Dumbledore as gay: '....because gay people just look like...people?' However, she's also seems to have implied that in order for a (wo)man to love another (wo)man, *sexuality* must be an element. Why does sexuality have to come into it at all?

A gay friend complained that in high school, he had difficulty in making friends with other men because they assumed that if he liked them, he wanted to bed them as well. His response was, 'you like women; do you want to sleep with every woman you like?' He was an immensely talented dancer, choreographer and wit, but because of one characteristic unrelated to everyday association, many refused him friendship.

Such a rejection is more commonplace than we'd like to think. How many friendships, homo- and hetero-sexual, have been denied because of the immature conviction that all relationships must result in sex? Shall we accept that the only reason two people can be friends is carnality? On one hand, the presumption speaks to individual fear; on another, individual conceit. It screams insecurity and naiveté. We have numerous examples of 'homosexual' interaction in a 'heterosexual' population—two buddies going to the pub for a pint after work for example, or two ladies who are business partners. By extension, when a group of friends decides to go to a concert or a game together, does that mean group sex will follow?

Heaven help the man or woman out walking the dog!

Rowling's announcement those many years ago was a good way to stir up her audience, and increase interest in her books and the films that followed. Concerning the stories themselves (about which we have perhaps forgotten by now), I have to ask:

Was it important? Did it add anything artistically to the saga? Is it genuinely newsworthy?

I'm much more interested, and much more uplifted, when someone points out that Sarah Michelle Gellar and Freddie Prinz Jr have been *happily married for thirteen years*!

These days, *that's* newsworthy!

※※※

Extremities
17 April 2015

Each time I consider the subject of Tolerance and Intolerance, I come to the same conclusions, no matter what in what direction I start. We live in a culture that revels in Extremes, and these Extremes strain our sensibilities. The greater the difference between our values and our realities, the greater the conflict and need for resolution.

The food industry seems to cater to extremes. You can go to a 'fine dining' restaurant and spend exorbitantly for a quantity of food that amounts to a smudge on your plate. In contrast, sandwich shops create sandwiches and hoagies that are so BIG you have to disarticulate your jaws to get the thing in your mouth (and every time you take a bite, half the contents spill into your lap). Comfort foods often have chemical effects on the body, reducing stress and creating that sense of comfort. A full stomach is always comforting. Still, we have a great national concern over obesity and 'unhealthy' diet. A lot of comfort foods are affordable, which is perhaps one more reason people are critical of the obese. If they had any 'class', they'd starve themselves in expensive restaurants. The more you spend for the less you get, the more the more you waste, the more affluent and impressive you seem.

Extremes are apparent in social attitude as well. Recently the news media have reported about Christian companies and individuals, refusing to serve people in same-sex relationships. Just this morning there was a report of a garage owner who refuses to serve gay couples, and gives a 10% discount to gun-owners. He is a 'Christian'. Jesus said something about the requirements for *casting the first stone*, and in another place, mentioned not judging *lest ye also be judged*. Although I'm sure it occurs in other religions, these protests are most noticeable in Christianity, with people using the religion based in part on *loving your neighbour as yourself* to excuse their own fears, insecurities, and prejudices.

Societal critics angrily descry extremes in governmental spending on war vs homelessness. Social service programmes pride themselves on 'helping the poor,' but only help the poor to remain poor; financial assistance doesn't cover even basic real-life expenses. Critics support rights to freedom of speech, bearing arms, etc, until someone actually exercises them. They proclaim the justice system until the courts do not support popular opinion of someone's guilt, then run riot.

What has this to do with tolerance?

The mistaken notion of tolerance is that it means approval, agreement, compliance, or membership. You can show tolerance for another culture, religion, lifestyle, or political attitude without agreeing, embracing, or having to be 'one of them'. Another connotation of tolerance is 'putting up with', so the person who is tolerant of racial equality or equal rights for women is risking a lot to say so, even when s/he means it in the most positive way. Tolerance doesn't mean putting up with something, it means letting something alone.

Tolerance and intolerance set boundaries, and the boundaries may have to be flexible. How rigid to you want to be when your priorities conflict with your standards? We must be clear about our boundaries without being judgemental. Our responsibility is not to make decisions and choices for other people, to impose our values on them, or decide whether they're good or evil, particularly when who or what they are has no bearing on who or what we are.

The world is big enough to make difference possible, and small enough to make tolerance (allowing differences to exist unmolested) necessary. If we could accept that point of view, we would be a much happier, peaceful and peaceable society. There is wisdom in the adage 'live and let live.'

The people you do not tolerate may not tolerate you either. What then?

◆-◆-◆

The Wedge
28 April 2015

What will you remember about me if I introduced myself to you as a man with green blood, and *then* mentioned I have interests in music, religion and spirituality, and the history of the Romanov dynasty? Which feature will remain foremost in your mind?

Unless you're a haematologist, the least relevant aspect of our relationship would be my green blood, but that's the characteristic you're most likely to recall because it's so odd. There are a lot of people who are interested in music, religion, and even the history of the Romanov Dynasty. You will always remember my green blood.

Having made this news public, I've not only distinguished myself as unusual, but I've made myself a little more difficult to relate to. You can't relate to 'green blood,' but you could find common ground in music. That 'label' separates me from the rest of the crowd, and if I really want to be unappreciated (because what use is green blood?), I won't keep it a secret. A rift begins to develop, which in time can become a chasm.

My reason for bringing this up is that in the media recently, celebrities have drawn attention to themselves for reasons that are no one's business but theirs, and probably of no real interest to anyone but themselves. What matters is not what religion they've turned to, their new diet, or whom they take as lovers—what matters is what they do. There are some people who seem to be famous only for being famous. The differences they announce don't 'create awareness', they simply draw attention, and may earmark them in later years. Someone may write the truly greatest novel of the century, but owing to a previous proclamation of difference, be known primarily for being the fellow who is 'a gerbil trapped in a hamster's body'.

Oddly enough, a couple of celebrities had elements of notoriety in their personal or ancestral past that they didn't want to bring to the public's attention—they favoured privacy—and that generated almost as much discussion as if they'd followed the examples of the attention-deprived and indiscreet. I'm sure that was not the result they wanted.

Of course, being ordinary is boring. No one will read a news release (in fact there would very likely never be such a release) in which a celebrity announces he is straight, she has not converted to a different religion, they are happily married, or that ancestrally, the family antecedents have always been on the boring side. A bit of difference and even notoriety is welcome, like seasoning in a stew, but as in all things, there must be BALANCE. There is such a thing as *too much*.

With so much attention given to differences, particularly when those differences are not especially relevant to other facts, it's much more challenging to find common ground. Every difference drives in the wedge. Some may feel that calling attention to a characteristic is creating awareness, but I believe it is merely the free advertising of something irrelevant that will garner them attention.

We like to think we are in a Global Village, and certainly with technological advancements, the world is effectively smaller than it used to be. As a Global

Village, we are often frightened by differences, to which many news items will attest. What might be commonly accepted in one culture is an anathema in another. Social morés change over time, but not globally. What was socially stigmatizing twenty years ago is routinely accepted to-day. Although world religions agree about many things, they also disagree about many other things, and do not soften the view that only they are right.

Perhaps it has been this way always, but we live in a society in which the prurient interests of the pathologically voyeuristic are fed, and good sense is not. Flexibility and acceptance (tolerance, if you like) are necessary, but we should remind ourselves that it is possible to go too far. Even the most flexible branch, if bent too far, will break.

We really need a global village. We need to find, and live on, common ground.

And for anyone who's interested, my blood is red.

✣✣✣

Random Acts of Kindness
4 May 2015

Last week there was a message on a celebrity's Facebook page, in the reply section of one of her entries. The person who posted this message offered words of encouragement to anyone who would read them, speaking of the reader's ability to be an inspiration, wishing the reader happiness, and reminding the reader that it is beautiful to be human. While it didn't belong where it was found, not a single person objected, and many commented on the uplifting effect it had on them. Would that there were more postings like that!

I follow several celebrities on Facebook and Twitter, attracted by their personal qualities and commitments rather than for their professional accomplishments. (Most of them I've never heard sing or seen act.) Several regularly promote and are active with charities devoted to a particular cause. Some take a more scattergun approach and support charities and causes that have nothing to do with one another, but still, they are drawing attention to worthwhile efforts to alleviate the suffering of fellow humankind. This is a positive use of the celebrity status.

Equally interesting are celebrities who have established charities of their own, or who have become Ambassadors for a particular need or population, and have pursued their responsibilities with utter devotion. I won't name the celebrities I admire—it would be far more useful for you to do your own research and make your own discoveries.

Another reason I don't name names is that many of my 'idols' number among the Great Unknown. You won't find their names on Wikipedia or Google Plus. Their accomplishments are done in privacy, and you wouldn't know their names if you heard them. Sometimes their kindnesses involve things like emptying a freezer of frozen food during a power failure, taking the food to the poorest section of town and giving it away. One young woman only has to smile and say 'hello' to fill a dismal day with sunshine. There is the single mother who supports an elderly neighbour with daily messages of inspiration and support and the occasional spaghetti dinner. There is a young person I heard about a year ago who made a list of ways to offer acts of kindness to total strangers, sometimes without ever meeting them. Encouraging notes were received by people whose names were in the telephone book, and others received loving messages in helium balloons launched from far away. I wish I remembered the details—there is a lot to be said about her.

A Franciscan missionary took great pleasure in doing things for his religious community, such as restoring an ancient electric lamp to usefulness, without revealing that he was the benefactor. His brother friars wondered who had donated this wonderful antique lamp—'we had something like it once'. There's a store clerk who will tell you, 'Don't buy this from me today—go across the street, they sell it for less. Next week, buy it here, because it will be on sale for less than they sell it now.'

When it comes to celebrities, it has been suggested it is unwise to meet your 'idols'. Such admiration often comes with an unrealistic expectation of perfection and nobility, and we forget that our idols are just as human, frail and flawed as the rest of us.

We can appreciate, and easily follow the examples of people such as these I have described. Spending money, or investing huge amounts of time, doesn't have be part of the act. Kindness might be as simple as listening to someone, or accepting their fears without making them feel inadequate. It might be a message in a balloon, or a posting on a Facebook page, a whisper, a smile and a nod at a stranger on the street....

It could even be judicious silence.

Acts of evil may please a few while they outrage and dismay others, but I've never heard of anyone objecting to an act of kindness.

✥✥✥

The Child is Father of the Man
22 May 2015

I have forgotten the delights of growing up. I'm generally not nostalgic; I have no desire to see people with whom I went to school, or visit old neighbourhoods. I did that once and found it a grave mistake. When I think about all the years behind me, I shudder and say, 'thank God *that's* done!'

Then I look at my neighbour's daughter, and I am reminded of some of the charming characteristics of the very early years. She's ten years old. We spend time together each day after school, and I watch her transform, sometimes too quickly, from child to teen. Sometimes I wish I could be more like she is.

There's a real joy to being a child; your head is full of ideas; there are things you want to do, places you want to explore, friends you want to see to-day. The days are full of adventure and discovery. There is a refreshing absence of inhibition that allows my little friend to dance interpretively to *every single ringtone* on my mobile telephone. The tiny 'witching voice' of mischief prompts the spontaneous composing of a song she calls 'Dancing with the Boogie Man'. It isn't until the very last chorus that you understand that the Boogie Man is not a minion of the Devil, but a man who boogie dances.

It will be a loss to the world when that little girl grows up, and I wish I could make her stay. It is difficult, though, because the word a child *should* hear the most often is 'yes', but the word a child *does* hear most often is 'no!' No, you have an upset stomach; you can't eat chili and ice cream. No, you can't ride your bicycle on the roof. No, you can't shake a bottle of champagne and watch the cork pop from an inch away. Being told 'no' urges a child to grow, leaving behind much of what we want to preserve and protect, until she can make choices without us.

They go to school to learn (because they have to—it isn't likely they would have chosen it for themselves). They learn what the teacher tells them, taking her lessons as gospel, even when she's wrong. You cannot unseat a child's confidence in her teacher!

A blessed compensation for school (from the child's point of view) is that they make friends with other children, but then, most of the time that they spend together, they aren't allowed to play because they have to be in class. Conflict after conflict between desire and rule, with no control over anything, always hearing 'no', rarely being right—sometimes they are even taught what to think, because it's faster than letting them work it out for themselves. I think it is very hard. I'm sure there's an alternative, but I can't imagine what alternative modern Adults would find acceptable.

In essence, a child is born as a beautiful, natural, blossoming plant, which we clip, shape, make grow the way *we* like, and maybe even jam into a pot. 'This child will be what we want it to be!' That doesn't work very well, does it? As we teach children to be more self-sufficient and capable, they become self-sufficient and capable in ways we do not like. They are defiant because they want to exercise the freedom with which they were born. Suitably squashed, disciplined, restrained, repressed, shaped and sculpted, a single child can guarantee long-term employment to a whole herd of therapists!

The Buddhists refer to 'the Original Face'; the Taoists talk about 'P'u—the Uncarved Block.' This was our natural state when we were born, before experiences— good and bad—began to shape us, mould us, pressing us into conformity. That fresh and original nature is what we seem to treasure most in children, while at the same time doing our best to stamp it out. A certain amount of shaping is necessary for the safety of the child, and we are adamant that people 'fit in' in our societies—individuality is praised and deplored in almost the same breath. It is good for a child to learn to read—think of the poetry and literature s/he would miss otherwise. A child should develop a good vocabulary, so as to better and more richly express her own ideas. It is unnecessary for a child to learn to sing, because she already sings songs like 'Dancing with the Boogie Man', and gives healthy expression to that 'witching voice' of mischief which delights us.

I wonder what we adults are missing. While we are teaching children to be industrious, are we missing the lesson they want us to learn—to play? As we tell them not to talk to strangers, are they telling us to be less distrustful? *Be wise as serpents and innocent as doves.* What can we learn from them—why must they only learn from us? What would happen if we allowed ourselves to be as unfettered as children?

William Wordsworth wrote, 'the Child is father of the Man'.

Honour your father.

✥✥✥

Forgiveness Part Two
3 June 2015

In a previous article, I mentioned that forgiveness benefits the forgiver—you have made a conscious effort to let go of bad feelings, and to not invest any more emotional energies that colour your point of view and drag you down. In doing so, you enable the wound to heal. Some acts, and some people, are easier to forgive than others, so this is entirely a subjective thing, and not subject to criticism from others. Others may have greater, or less, difficulty in forgiving than you do. It is very individual.

We respond with anger. It's part of the 'fight or flight' response that is embedded in our brains (the amygdala is responsible). This is a very primal response—when threatened, we respond with a show of strength and menace. Although our hair no longer stands on end, and we do not bellow and beat our chests, the feeling of anger gives us a (false) sense of power and control. No one is less in control of him/herself than an enraged person.

We also respond with sadness. Duplicity hurts. Kahlil Gibran wrote that our pain is the breaking of the shell that encloses our understanding. This too is natural—we mourn what is missing in our lives.

A certain amount of anger and resentment are natural, even necessary. Our response to an injury validates us. We tell ourselves we do not deserve to be slighted or injured, that we are worthy of better than we have been given. Others may try to explain, justify, or offer alternative points of view. Although they aren't siding with the person who hurt you, it might feel that way. What they need to do for now is listen.

A component of forgiveness is understanding. First, understand that although you are affected, the problem isn't necessarily yours. While we realize everyone has problems, it often takes us by surprise when we see the problems of other people played out in front of us. It's like dealing with someone with chronic bad breath—although your nose is offended, the problem is his. In Poland, they say, *Nie mój cyrk, nie moje małpy* ('Not my circus, not my monkey'). Things that happen are not always your fault or responsibility, and this is important to remember. We have too many real responsibilities to take on undeserved blame.

Some people are constitutionally incapable of fair play, honesty, or respect of personal boundaries. Forgiving someone doesn't 'let them off the hook', but if you don't forgive them, the act can continue to affect you long after it's over. Whether or not you pursue the matter, the person who stole from you is still a thief; the one who struck you is still a thug. Such vile behaviour seems to them to be the most advantageous solution. It's in their nature to be the way they are. I am thinking of a man who did a great deal of harm to others by lying and distorting facts. It took a while to recognize, and even longer to accept. I never understood why he did the things he did, or how he benefitted from his behaviour, but I do understand this is his way—he'll never change, and should be regarded with caution.

I am also thinking of people during my social service career who acted in ways that were upsetting and disruptive to others. I knew their histories, and it was apparent that their actions were meant to preserve their physical and mental well-being as they understood 'well-being' to be. After recognizing they weren't able to act differently, it was easier to forgive their actions. Yes, everyone has a choice, but when you know nothing else, your options obviously are limited.

Another aspect of forgiveness really doesn't involve the person who hurt you; here, the focus is you! You can't move on until you've accepted that something bad really has happened. In 2011, my home burnt down. It took a very long time to accept that my world had been turned upside down—nothing I knew of normalcy applied anymore. It's no different when someone is an identifiable cause. When you allow the pain of the event to recede, when you can allow that something awful really happened, then you are ready to forgive and move on.

As was mentioned in the last article, forgiving someone doesn't mean you have to keep allowing yourself to be hurt. I came across a quote, the source of which I can't trace, that said in effect, when you bear an injury and allow nothing in the relationship to be changed, that is true forgiveness. This is a very idealistic definition. As people, we hurt and we remember. Injury will change us, even if only to make us a bit more cautious, until we are certain we can trust again.

Our part in forgiveness is to direct that change.

Reversible Spelling
17 June 2015

I've been busy with a variety of writing projects lately, including articles for clients, for myself, co-authoring an eBook on exercise related abdominal cramps, and at least one book I hope to put up for publication by the end of the summer. My brain has begun complaining of fatigue. 'I've been working and working for you. Feed me!' (Yes, my brain talks to me.)

If you want to trawl the internet for linguistic entertainment, there's really no better place to start than the Home page of your Google Plus account. Pay attention to the Spam folder as well, for you can find great riches there (just not the sort of riches the sender intended).

Exploration began with an article about Winners and Loosers. There was spam mail from a general contractor whose services included 'floor striping' and 'dinning room refinishing'. There was an invitation from SweatCandi to visit her personal webpage. She described herself as a real cutty with nice bobbs, who liked to take her clothing of. Opps, don't tell anyone!

CNN.com can often be relied on for a linguistic chuckle. There was an article about the Ex-Egyptian President. Well, he was an Egyptian before, what is he now? (A writer of my acquaintance once wrote something about an ex-Hispanic consumer, and was chagrined when I suggested the consumer was probably still Hispanic.)

I wish there *were* a technique for loosing weight—it would be faster and much easier than all that dieting. And perhaps we have leapt to a conclusion, and the contractor specialises in bowling alleys, and noisy rooms.

These are simple mistakes to make. Being something of a purist when it comes to language, my concern is that English is one of the most beautiful languages in the world, and this sort of carelessness threatens the integrity of our tongue. (There's another one, 'tounge'!) We really need to pay attention to how we write, before a precedent is established.

This week I posted on Facebook a humorous picture I'd found on Pinterest. It said 'Your the best teacher ever!' I mentioned two teacher friends in the comment section, and they went to town on me. The first one thanked me and said I should have known better that to write 'your' instead of 'you're'. I said it was a joke. The second teacher commented that I spelt 'joke' right, so at least I was paying attention to 'grammer'. I corrected that ('grammar'), and the first teacher remarked, 'It was a JOKE.' These two women have never met, so either they share professional solidarity on a psychic level, or they're part of the same coven. If they know my high school geometry teacher, I vote for the latter.

These examples led me to wonder how it would be if the same mistakes were made, but in the opposite direction? (I've had to take some liberties here, so please pardon me.)

I suppose someday we'll be treated to a story about a girl who volunteers at hospital as a candy stripper, and who sweets during exercise. Her father drinks Cutey Sark. Her brother's name is Boob. They meet at the dinner for diner once a week. Her mother is on a diet and her clothing is loser. There's an uncle no one talks about because he's a spy, working in Clandestine Oops. He's so mysterious no one ever knows what he's thinking off.

I hope I've made my point.

╬╬╬

Chain of Events
5 July 2015

I would like to announce that the Global Village is under attack from within. The chief participants in this assault are the Pathologically Narcissistic, the Morbidly Voyeuristic, and of course, the Idiopathic Opinionated. You may think of them as the Army, the Arms Dealers, and the Press, respectively.

'Pathological' because there's a little bit of each in every person. It's actually healthy to think well of yourself, to be curious about others, and to live according to your beliefs, like, and dislikes in order to establish a safe living environment. If I don't want the word 'pathological', perhaps I mean 'morbid' in its medical sense—it's unhealthy, and 'idiopathic' is easy to explain—of unknown origin.

In the last month or so, there have been numerous revelations that have driven the public into at least two camps. I will not discuss (and I've purposely left it late to bring up) either of my two examples: the Jenner transgender announcement, and the SCOTUS decision on same-sex marital unions. Jenner's announcement had to do with *gender identity*, while the SCOTUS decision was about *civil rights, due process*, etc. Neither of these were about *sex*, but the public seemed to make that association almost immediately; *sex* is exciting and 'dirty', and a short step to *perversion*, something we deplore and can't hear enough about. The stage is set for inflammatory commentary.

Those in support heralded the announcement and the court decision as breaking the chains of oppression and prejudice; the world, the nation, the society are emerging into a new age of enlightenment. They revelled in the freedom to love whom they, or others, wished to love, and in whatever manner (although neither was never an issue).

Those against said the world is coming to an end and God hates us.

Each point of view triggered a chain of events. One actress was so enthusiastic about the SCOTUS decision, she posted so many 'yippees' on social network pages (first link)—that her public began to complain (second link). This generated responses (third link) from other followers defending the actress and her passion, and by the tenth link, they weren't discussing SCOTUS or the actress any more, they were publicly abusing each other online.

Those opposed did much the same. In chatrooms I read about the world coming to an end, the country is going down the tubes, the approbation of perversion, and God being disappointed. There was lively debate for a while, but eventually it too degenerated into a denominational and personal slanging match, with prior generations being blamed for setting the stage for this disaster. Scriptural supports for varying points of view were cited, and a lot of opinions were offered as gospel. (As with many sources, with judicious selection and editing, the Bible can be made to support anything you like.)

A year ago I was peripherally involved with a military PTSD online support group, and the same thing happened. A discussion about ISIS, or the government's failure to support veterans invariably turned into free publicity *for* ISIS (in the form of protest against ISIS), and undermined support for the military and the country generally, with nasty commentary on previous commentators.

In whatever camp you find yourself, and regardless of the Cause you're supporting, it isn't long before the chain of events is hardly related to the anchor point—the announcement or the decision—at all. With each new link, animosity and insistence grow, until one has the impression of a massive, online bar fight. We've all been in arguments that start with, 'get your spoon out of my soup', and before long, with a chorus of '*and another thing!*' closely resemble high school rumbles.

Losing sight of the original intention, being heedless of the difference between opinion and information, and often, being unblemished by actual fact, we find ourselves boiling over about (as happened in these examples) something which affects very few of us directly. Angry views push perspective out the window.

If we are all the fine things we believe we are, if we are 'wise' enough to have opinions, we are wise enough to handle this much better. We might also save ourselves a great deal of bother if we were to stop indulging the Narcissistic and the Voyeuristic.

Do you know what the Bible says?

> *Greet one another with a holy kiss.*
> *2 Corinthians 13:12*

✣✣✣

What Next?
24 July 2015

I promise not to mention my new book in this article. Not a word about the new book. In fact, WHAT new book entitled *Behind These Red Doors: Stories A Cathedral Could Tell Volume 2,* available on Amazon.com? I have no idea to what you're referring. Perhaps you're overwrought and should read a good book. How about *Behind These Red Doors: Stories A Cathedral Could Tell Volume 2?* Just a thought.

But now that the secret messages have been imbedded in the text, and all the typos are part of the historic tapestry of Literature, I have more free time than usual on my hands, and I'm feeling a little panicky. We are inclined to define ourselves in Western Civilization by what we do, and the loss of structure or purpose (or in my instance, the need for repurposing) removes some of the structure to which we're accustomed. It's actually uncomfortable to wake up in the morning and realize you have absolutely no idea what you're going to do to-day. It poses a zen-like question: if I have no purpose at the moment, do I still exist?

Perhaps this is one reason people keep themselves so busy—so long as they're moving and *doing something*, they show proof of life. As soon as they stop—poof! they're gone!

In a way, it's true—our inactivity encourages people to forget us; friendships and business relationships thrive on continuous and frequent interaction. Our self-identity relies on what we're doing. A musician moved from Philadelphia to New England, returning to Philadelphia for a visit a few years later. He ran into an old acquaintance he hadn't seen in a long time, and received this greeting: 'I thought you were dead!'

A Franciscan missionary told me that one of the first things he noticed when he went to Papua New Guinea was that the people there asked different questions when they first meet someone. *Are you married? Do you have children?* Of course, as a Franciscan priest, he didn't have much to tell them. However, it was a pleasant change not to be defined solely by his job.

It might be more interesting, if it's actually necessary to do so, to be defined by our interests or non-professional activities, but it seems unlikely this would find acceptance. 'How do you do, I'm a pipe smoker', or 'My name is John and I collect Sherlock Holmes memorabilia.' It would certainly be more interesting than 'I'm a lawyer,' simply because everyone knows what a lawyer is and does. No one has to ask questions, and the simple answer becomes a conversation killer.

There are times when a specific identifier is important. When you view websites like About.me, often people define themselves so fluidly that you have no idea what they're about. How does a 'karmalogist' make a living? What the heck is an 'immortalist'? These titles encourage exploration and conversation, but they may also encourage people to create a title for you: 'Nutter!'

I suppose how we identify ourselves depends on what we think other people will value. Western society, with its influence on societies around the world, is obsessed with making money. We are defined by how we make money. Perhaps by saying, 'I'm an accountant,' we are hoping to attract clients, ie: make more money.

I'm a person who spends his time thinking about things, asking weird questions such as 'What is the essential difference between strength and power?', and then writing whatever I've been thinking. I watch a lot of DVDs, read books, listen to ragtime music (piano only), write with a fountain pen, and drink Diet Coke by the bucket. I think you know me a lot better than if I'd said, 'Writer.'

Okay, that's that. Now I'm going to read. Can anyone suggest a good book?

☩☩☩

Old and Grey
29 July 2015

I can hear the footsteps on the path, chasing me along the way. As I run, on either side, branches seem to reach out to clutch at me, to cling to me, tear at my hair, and arrest my flight. I narrowly escape their grasp though they slash at me.

Overhead, the almost-black sky lowers threateningly, adding to my sense of haste, my need to fly before my pursuer. My heart is pounding in my chest and roaring in my ears as the thunder resounds around me. My lungs gasp for air, and perspiration pours into my eyes almost like a cataract, as does the rain. I must stay the course, I must continue my escape. I must remain ahead of the one who is running after me.

The wind howls, and behind me, my pursuer shrieks like a banshee. Lashings of rain crash against my old grey head—my old, grey, head. I am, so I have been told, *old*.

It was just yesterday that I was speaking to someone on the telephone. I was asking for his professional help because it is not just the hellion behind me that follows me, but time itself. He asked my age, and I said 'Sixty years', and he told me, 'you are old.'

If I were an Islay single-malt whiskey (which I could use right about now), I would be pleasantly 'old', much sought after, and at great price. If I were a star, a glistening light in the heavens, I would be a mere infant and you would not be able to detect me for thousands of years. At sixty years, I have seen the first man walk on the moon, and mourned the death of great leaders; I have 'seen pale kings and princes,' and attended the premiere performances of symphonies. History has grown around me, always adding to the length of its days. Because I am 'old.'

The screams and cries behind me are closing in. The footsteps are drawing near. I must press on. I must not be caught!

The man assumed because I am old, therefore I am stupid. His tone of voice changed, and he forsook his education to simplify his speech. Because I am 'old', I easily recognized his patronizing arrogance and condescension, and yes, I was offended. My impatience with his arrogance was taken for the ignorance of dotage. His presumption to sophistication did not equip him well enough to recognize how offensive he was. He had not seen what I have seen, nor did he have the benefit of time to recognize the difference between attitude and real wisdom. If I am 'old', I am old enough to recognize that the wisdom of my years does not amount to much—wise the one who know how wise he is not.

The number of questions I have has grown with the passing of the years. I chase the answers, which flee before me.

I don't deny that age has touched me. Time has bestowed upon me the winter crown of silver hair and a white beard. I am no longer as fleet of foot as I once was. The number of new friends and new experiences dwindles as the count of past relationships and memories grows. People seek me out less frequently, preferring newer, fresher fare. I may not be as young as I think I am, but I also am not as old as you think I am.

The thunder of feet is behind me, approaching. I can almost feel hot breath and the clutch of cold fingers. I must away! Vainly I attempt to increase my pace. Because I am 'old', and have the wealth of accumulated experience, I know *this* much:

If that kid gets home before me in this storm, there won't be a dry towel in the entire house, and I'll be soaking wet all afternoon!

✛✛✛

Dances Sacred and Profane
11 August 2015

Social media sites like Facebook and Pinterest (and to some extent LinkedIn) are grand for taking the pulse of the people and measuring change over time. Not only individuals, but potential employers/clients consult these pages to research people in whom they have an interest. As a freelance writer and consultant, I want to put my best foot forward, and my prospective clients see these pages as well. What must they think?

I occasionally look at the pages of people I once knew because I am curious about their progress. I recently visited the page of a young woman who once worked for me as a temp. Back then, she was vain, self-absorbed and immodest. Her earliest photos displayed her revealing clothing, and usually she was in the company of an open bottle shared with equally immodest friends. I always had the impression they'd been photographed in the back alley of a sleazy nightclub. Recently I looked at her page again. Unruly photographs have been replaced with photos of her children and her family—she rarely appears in the photographs she posts. In those in which she has appeared, she is tastefully attired without having lost any of her appeal, and she has obviously matured without losing her sparkling personality. She would be very welcome if the occasion arose.

In contrast, I came across the page of a young woman whose father I had known. She was a cute four-year-old when I met her. I got a look at her page recently. Now in her 20s, she has surpassed her parents in body-ink and piercings, and her language, attitude and apparent interests are crude and vulgar. She is no longer the sweet four-year-old I met. If approached, I would scream and run for cover. She's left a horrible impression.

In a recent conversation, a woman with a home business mentioned she uses her Facebook page to reach out to customers. It is the same page she uses to post pictures of family picnics, and share non-business related information with friends. It isn't exactly helping her, because there are times when viewers can't tell the business from the personal postings.

I myself have had some difficulty with the content that ends up on my Facebook and Pinterest pages. With the best will in the world, there are people who post 'motivational' and 'inspirational' content that ranges from supportive to saccharin, to practically fanatical. These sometimes end up where others can see them.

I have a difficulty with the other end of the spectrum too. I find postings of a political (practically abusive) nature, and sometimes postings on topics that wouldn't be suitable in most venues, with language that is absolutely foul. These wind up on my pages too. So I repeat, what must my prospective clients think?

So whether its Facebook or Pinterest (and on some occasions LinkedIn too), I seem to be providing a neutral ground for the Dance of Sacred and Profane. Unless I want to severely dismantle my social network, I'm at a bit of a loss. There are things that only I see, and wish I didn't have to—I wanted to know and share a bit of people's lives, but they seem to be interested in showing me the least desirable parts. And then there are the postings which circulate without control—websites favoured by other people that wind up on my pages.

I fully support freedom of self-expression. As the world more and more becomes a global village, self-expression is influential. We never know who sees what we do, or how what we post affects the thinking or feelings of others about us. We can't know how it has affected our prospects.

It seems that without doing harm to our social and images and personal relationships, we cannot prevent our friends from doing harm to us.

How about some restraint and consideration?

✦✦✦

A Glimmer of Light
21 August 2015

My last article had to do with some of the things that wind up on my Social Media pages—strident, foul, maniac expressions of opinion, abrasiveness and greed. I spend more time 'hiding this post' on Facebook and whizzing past similar assaults to sensitivity on Pinterest, than I do reading what remains. My protests seem to have fallen on blind eyes and deaf ears—if anything such postings have increased in number.

The brutal cudgelling by political 'right', the lash from the whip of religious 'righteousness', and the putrid filth that emanates from coarse language seem to be echoes of everyday living. There are so many people to whom a promise is a joke and commitment a failing, and whose aim is to get as much as they can for as little as they can give, and do so with a smile. People dedicated to serving others have lost their way; programmes and forms are more important than people. Many of us feel the intensity of day-to-day assault-without-violence (although there's plenty of violence too). I am sick of it; I am sickened *by* it.

There are tiny glimmers of agreeable contradiction—someone who gives more than gets, who reaches out before being summoned, who accepts a challenge despite its inherent difficulties. These glimmers are comforting and fill dark places. I actually thrill to someone saying 'I don't know what to say,' rather than feigning understanding, wisdom and genius. Such honesty is treasured.

Last year I posted two articles, 'Ring the Bell' and 'Ring the Bell II', in which I expressed a very earnest desire: *'Somewhere in the universe, someone needs to ring a bell, and all this friction and conflict will stop. We will all put away our disagreements, hostilities and strife, go for a beer, and spend a pleasant evening.'* The articles were well-received; in fact, they are the two most-revisited articles I've published. They offered a rather Utopian alternative, and the growing number of readers and re-readers suggests a desire, perhaps even a passionate starvation, for solace.

And why not? Would you like to exchange the vomit of vitriolic hearts, the decay of hate-filled thoughts, and the cat-o'-nine-tails comfort of dogma for something embracing, loving and uplifting? Do the violence of opinion, superiority and violation find a welcoming place in your life? Is there just one tiny glimmer of light?

Like the sun rising over the shore, the glimmer begins to spread across the sea and the land. The ocean waves rush up onto the vast expanse of sand, bathing and smoothing. Cold harsh darkness slowly warms and wanes as daylight tenderly explores the shadowy places, even the tiniest crevices. It is harder to feel alone in the Light. Light comes from something; darkness stands alone.

The sea sings a consoling song in every key and every language, and the music of the water is a caress to the empty heart and aching soul. Although children of earth, we began in the wet. The clammy sand of night dries and warms; it is soft enough to conform to us, and firm enough to hold us up. Ocean breezes tease us, ruffling our hair, and stroking our faces and bodies. We can close our eyes, not to hide from, but to savour *everything*. We can run, not to flee, but to play. We can chase the waves, and they in turn will chase us with mischievous tenderness. If we have tears, they will mingle with the deep to be carried away. If we have laughter, it will be borne upon the wind and spread abroad. Laughter is contagious.

It is here that we will thrive, and here we will heal. It is here we will be free of harsh words, encountering nothing more imposing than wind and water and light.

There may be no bell that is rung, calling for an interruption to discord. There may be only a glimmer of light.

Light *overcomes* darkness.

I wish you peace.

⊹⊹⊹

The Author's Dilemma
13 September 2015

A friend recently asked me, 'Why should I read your books? I mean, if I didn't know you, if I weren't your friend, why would I read your books?'

I imagine every author believes s/he has something to say, a tale to tell. Through the skilful weaving of thoughts and dreams, by way of masterfully artistic use of the English language, s/he has something to offer the rest of the world. I believe that myself. If there's no such thing as an 'original idea—it's all been thought of before', there's always a new way of saying something in hopes of stimulating a positive reaction in the reader. There is the added benefit of sharing something of oneself, of opening oneself to others in hopes that by sharing ideas and dreams, others might better like, love, appreciate and/or understand the author as a person.

My books are listed at the end of this article, and you can click on the links to study them for yourself. *Lives of the Ain'ts: Comedic Biographies of Directors Errant* is a collection of faux-biographies. Almost all of the people are fictional, and their stories are utter nonsense! Don't we need a bit of nonsense in our lives? Something that draws laughter without causing pain, insult or humiliation? I originally wrote those stories to offer a bit of comic relief to the Annual Meetings of a facility of which I used to be Executive Director. If people were laughing *at* me, at least I gave them a comfortable reason—I was being intentionally silly, and adding a spirit of fun in the midst of ponderous material usually brought forward in an Annual Meeting of the Board of Directors. Everyone enjoys a good laugh, and it doesn't have to be at anyone's expense.

The Inn of Souls is about a professor who rented an old Inn for a summer, intending to write another scholarly book. He found the Inn occupied by the spirits of a number of people who had lived and died in different times, each of whom had his/her own story, had made mistakes, or lived with misconceptions. I was very excited about this book because the idea came as a spark one night, and I thought, 'I'd better write that down before I forget.' Before I realized it, it was 3 AM and I'd written fifteen pages! People I told about the book were fascinated by the idea of a 250-year-old ghost of a five-year-old girl who was at once the youngest and oldest person at the Inn. People like to hear the stories of others—sometimes it's an entertaining distraction, and other times, offers insight into some element of their own characters. Humour shakes up thinking because it has an element of surprise.

To me, my 'greatest work' (possibly because it's also the most recent work) is *Behind These Red Doors: Stories a Cathedral Could Tell.* It's in two volumes (the second being the most recently published), and it relates stories and experiences of people who have visited this Cathedral in the course of more than a century. It speaks of problems, and of hope. It offers different ways of perceiving situations, and I hope encourages thoughtfulness in the reader.

Someone told me, 'I'm a practicing Atheist; I don't think I'd be interested your book since its chief character is God.' I think, though, that he might, because even without the theological component, there's a lot that can be learnt, or enjoyed, in those stories. Sometimes the best solution to a problem is simply not to be alone. At other times, the best solution is to sit quietly and be still.

Without being pathologically voyeuristic, we can look at the lives of others and be entertained. We can be motivated, and sometimes enlightened, by the fact that no *problem* is original—they've all been had before. We can awaken feelings or dreams we'd forgotten we had, or recognize ourselves in someone else.

That's why you should read my books!

✣✣✣

The Blood Moon
28 September 2015

I suppose you may say that I am a creature of the night. Certainly, in any 24-hour period, I experience greater peace in the night time. Night time is excellent for study, for prayer, for contemplation, for creative pursuits. Whatever the burdens of the day, they are unlikely to disturb the night. The darkness enfolds me like a blanket. Night time is *my* time.

I must force myself to rise and enter the daylight world—we must live in the world we have, not the world we want. Daylight is a time of violence of every description, some of it productive, some of it not. Perusing social and news media, what do we see? Crimes are reported in brutal detail. Politicians and political hopefuls, celebrities, dignitaries of note make pronouncements that are ill-conceived, misunderstood, or twisted to make someone else's point. People post and repost terribly biased articles on social media that do not inform, but inflame, for purposes I cannot fathom. Reason has been sacrificed to ego-driven passion and rant. They claim to be concerned about the world they are helping to distress. I suspect they rarely read the articles they post, relying on misleading headlines. They will never have the peace and order they claim to desire, so long as they fan flames of discord and distrust.

I do not like the day. It is a time of industry, yes, but agitation, inane speeches, and getting one-up on your fellow beings. When I see and read what's happening in the day, I am very uncomfortable.

Last evening, the world was given a singular opportunity to observe a celestial event—the eclipse of the Blood Moon. I found it very exciting—like millions of others on the Earth, I was witnessing a carefully choreographed, completely natural, cosmic dance, one made despite the people watching. Inconceivably vast bodies moved through the heavens, bowed and curtsied. The Moon allowed the Earth to veil her face. No matter how warlike, opinionated or contentious the people on the earth, celestial orbs had their dance.

Bow, curtsy, move on.

It was thrilling to see something that was so far outside human power and control. We could only watch and feel awe. Some look to the heavens for answers— guidance, fate, and for some, perspective. No matter how tumultuous things become *here*, up *there*, there is peace.

My neighbours and I went out onto the patio roof to watch this minuet of Earth and Moon. We took photographs (and I learnt a few things about my old Nikon that I had not known). We watched the shadow of the world slowly edge across the lunar face. We saw the white light of the moon turn red, gliding across the sky in an arc, and become white again—just in time for bed.

I stayed out the latest of all of us, and celebrated this wonderful event. I drank a little champagne, and considered that what we had seen brought things into perspective—at least for me. My celebration was silent and cerebral, but full of joy and awe. I think we were meant to feel awe, and be reminded there are things far greater than we.

There was a celebration that I valued more—one I am too old and too stuffy to join. My neighbour's daughter, who has just entered the fifth grade, sings and dances at the drop of a hat. Last night, she sang and danced in the light of the Blood Moon. 'It's a *red* moon,' she sang, 'it's a *red* moon, it's a R.E.D (breath) M.O.O.N.' and gleefully danced in the light of something as innocent and astonishing as she. *Out of the mouths of babes....*

I would rather celebrate than fight. I would rather find peace than argue about it. I do not want to impose myself on you, as you do on me. I would like to be like the moon and just *be*.

An interesting note: this morning, when I made my customarily hesitant review of social media and news websites, there were fewer outrageous and inflammatory postings. Perhaps I was not the only one to find perspective last evening.

Perhaps we all danced and put aside our mindless squabbles for the nonce.

✣✣✣

Transitions
26 October 2015

Plato had a lot to say about change: *Everything changes and nothing stands still.* And: *You could not step twice into the same river.* We don't always remember that transitions are irreversible, even when it seems they aren't. You can always change your mind and go back on a decision, but what you go back to won't be the same as what you've left. Everything we touch, everything we do, leaves a mark.

My contemplation on change is prompted by my having just moved to another part of the country. I've spent a lot of time reminiscing—it is a way of keeping things alive, and recalling my motivations. It's important to remember the past because it is the foundation of everything else you do and understand. The past offers concrete justification for my choices.

I can't forget the positive influences I found in the place I have just left. The friend/mentor who encouraged me in my freelance pursuits, for example— I wouldn't want to forget him. How about the neighbour friend with the magic spaghetti dinners, and her ten-year-old daughter who was often an inspiration and a joy? That friend went to great lengths to help me with my move, and it led to a shedding of tears for us both when it came time to part ways. In difficult times, she had a simple faith that 'things will work out,' and they invariably did. It's a lesson I struggle with, but it was 'things working out' that brought me from the Old to New World. Her daughter reminded me of the importance of simplicity—sometimes the answer to 'why' is simply 'because'. She thinks outside the box, spontaneously composes songs such as 'Dancing with the Boogie Man', and asks 'What do you think Jesus does on His breaks?' (A reasonable question for a parochial school student, yes?)

After my departure, my young friend looked within and wrote an eloquent and very frank account of how it feels to a ten-year-old to lose a close friend. *Sometimes what a person does leaves a big mark in our hearts* (she wrote), *but when they leave it's like someone ripped out our hearts and took it so we could never love.*

Transitions are inevitable. We grow, we change, we adapt or we languish and die. We need to look within; our satisfactions and dissatisfactions motivate us. My leaving was painful for her, and was an inevitable lesson. The favourite teacher, the beloved grandparent, the family pet, the best friend—they will leave at some point. Lessons of impermanence are brutal. They are accompanied by an equally painful awakening—we may do things for the benefit of others that hurt us. *We packed you up and loaded you into a van, and sent you away because we love you.* I confess it is an expression of love that makes me think twice before I recognize its value.

Transitioning is complex. It entails risk, entering the unknown, and sacrifice. No one escapes it, few enjoy it, but it is a large part of life. When we make that choice to change, it can have an impact on others, whether we like it or not. Surprisingly, things do work out; the pain of loss is comparatively brief, the fear of risk and change passes—all because of an additional choice—to move forward.

The past will always be with us. The lessons we learnt, the joys and sorrows we experienced, will leave a big mark in our hearts, and actually, the pain we feel is something we feel because we love, and want to continue loving. My young friend wasn't wrong, but she's ten and will learn someday there is a future, and things get better, and she will love again.

As her mother said, 'things will work out.'

✣✣✣

After It's Over
3 November 2015

For much of my life, I've been an absolutely crap cook. I could burn anything. Once, I put a frozen hamburger patty in my skillet and in three minutes had an *almost* thoroughly burnt disk of meat—there was one area that was raw and still frozen. They don't teach that in culinary classes—that requires talent!

Lately, I've been participating in the preparation of meals for the people with whom I am staying. I've developed some sensitivity and patience in the kitchen. They actually like my cooking. My hostess ate my fruit omelette and enjoyed it. Others to whom I have offered this culinary adventure have paled and declined. My hosts have also eaten my beef kebab, enjoyed something with shrimp and rice, and consumed a few other gustatory treats I'll share with you for tons of money—I prefer Euros in multiples of 100.

With these successes under my belt, if you'll pardon the expression, I recall a couple of accidental kitchen triumphs when I was at university, long ago. I worked in the Foreign Student Office, and many of my friends were from Asia. I learnt some simple recipes, including wonton soup and something my friend called Vietnamese Chicken Salad.

My girlfriend's mother invited me to the family estate to prepare wonton soup, and provided all the ingredients. Mom had bought a large quantity of pork *sausage* meat, which is already spiced and herbed and was unsuitable for this recipe. She was a little hurt when I asked as diplomatically as possible, 'Are you nuts?' but covered her discomfort well: 'Nuts? Was I supposed to get those?'

A year later, I trotted out the Vietnamese Chicken Salad for my parents. The ingredients are simple—shredded roast chicken, a salted head of cabbage and an onion, chopped and mixed well, then topped with a fish sauce mixture and peanuts. My father was allergic to fish and couldn't have the sauce, so he decided to spice up his plate with *cheddar cheese*. Horrible! East is East, West is West, and they have no business meeting on his dinner plate!

My current hosts eat my cooking with enjoyment, but some of their embellishments occasionally raise an eyebrow. Peanuts instead of sunflower kernels, for example (sunflower seeds have a more subtle flavour). Cole slaw is limited in its suitability, but in the Southern US, I am apparently a minority. (I have also learnt that in southern culture, if they don't say 'this is good' more than twice, they hate it.)

As an artist, I once sent a pair of paintings to a dentist in Japan. One was of his pet rabbit, the other of a cat. He liked the rabbit painting and gave it pride of place in his house. The cat painting he used to cover a water stain in his mother-in-law's hallway. Other paintings have received arcane interpretations, discussing imagery and significances I swear are not there. My poetry has been interpreted by people who are apparently from other planets. Some people make a living doing this—they are called 'critics', people who can neither do nor teach.

I was dining at a very popular Japanese restaurant when three men, seated at the table next to mine, ordered miso soup as their appetizer. Miso soup is a little salty because it is made from soy beans, and has a pleasant, delicate flavour. Without tasting it first, they *salted* and *peppered* their (salty) miso soup, then added *soy sauce* (also salty), and solemnly enjoyed their 'good food.' It was enough to make you weep (more salt—tears).

I have learnt that you can do your best, offering your finest work, but you cannot make people appreciate what you have done. You cannot control what people do with/to your creations. The work we do often is a vehicle or mechanism from which someone else will build. The question is, will they do so with judgement and wisdom? If the answer is 'no', do you serve them again without offending your creative integrity?

Dita von Teese, the Queen of Burlesque, once said: *You can be the ripest, juiciest peach in the world, and there's still going to be somebody who hates peaches.*

And I, who dance not at all, add: *No matter what you do or how well you do it, there will always be someone to use or enjoy your work in ways you never intended, considered, or wanted. That's their choice. You've done your job.*

What do you make of that?

✣✣✣

Trust
2 December 2015

What is trust? The dictionary defines it as confidence, reliance on a future outcome, or hope. I think, though, that these words are incomplete. There are essential qualities these words do not convey.

We have had many reasons to think about trust recently. Locally or internationally, much has happened to nurture our distrust, feed our fear and threaten our instinct for survival (even when we are not realistically imperilled). We've decided we can't trust foreigners, immigrants, politicians, clergy, and (insert your preference here), at home or abroad. We do this because we are afraid, because we do not trust.

One essential quality of trust is the absence of fear.

In Florida there is a young woman who is a light in dark places. She has an amazing number of 'friends' and 'followers' on Facebook. During the recent outrages in Europe and the Middle East, and the turmoil surrounding refugees coming to the US, she was positive and encouraging. She spoke against fear. I haven't met her, but I trust her. People such as she make trust a wonderful thing. The reason is that she radiates Love, and if she fights at all, it is *against* fear. Fear is the gift antagonists would like to give us.

The type of person who propounds negativity, who is misinformed and vocal, spreads hatred and fear. S/he spews bias and delusion, and whether you agree or not, your reaction is negative. When distrust and fear are sown, you are likely to feel hostility, if not for what is said, then perhaps for who said it. People who spread such hostile sentiment play right into the hands of those whom they oppose—they provide 'free advertising' and spread a gospel of hatred and fear through protest and denunciation.

No one's life is free from the taint of distrust. Children tell fibs, friends break promises, leaders deceive—we all have experience with broken trust. We become wiser, 'as serpents', and lose some of our dove-like innocence. The damage is done. The person who is distrustful causes others to feel ill-at-ease, and they become distrustful of him. If trust is a kind of love, then we've learnt to love less.

What benefit is there in spreading hatred and false belief? Hatred breeds hatred. The benefit to spreading love is clear—that woman in Florida has *8000+* friends and followers. The people who leave comments on her postings are unanimously positive and loving. Celebrities and personalities who have a positive message have vast followings, and long careers. They are popular because they are positive and bring out positive qualities in others.

Once trust is broken, it is difficult to restore. Trust is like a living thing—you can't turn it on and off like a lamp. If you break it, it is never fully restored, and possibly, never can be. Not only is it difficult to trust someone who has let you down, that experience leads you to greet new acquaintances with distrust. You would like to believe them. You would like to think them sincere and their words true, but unhappy experience tells you this is unwise. Distrust breeds distrust. If we distrust profoundly enough and long enough (encouraging others to distrust us), eventually we may not trust ourselves either, by second guessing—'this is my choice, but is it the right choice? I have erred before.'

We need to start somewhere. We need to decide what sort of people, religion, country we want to be. Trust doesn't occur instantly, it has to be earned, but it's disadvantageous for all involved when earning trust requires first removing distrust and suspicion. If we cannot begin by trusting, might we not begin by not distrusting? Can we take a neutral position and wait for evidence to show us how to feel, how to proceed?

In which world do you wish to live?

> *'Who trusts little is little trusted.'*
> --Lao Tse, *Tao Teh Ching* Ch 23

✢✢✢

Let's Lynch Lucy!
12 December 2015

The poet Ogden Nash wrote the poem 'Lucy Lake', about a woman who had an incredibly upbeat outlook on things. She was what some people term, 'a Pollyanna,' someone who is overly optimistic. Nash wrote about Lucy: *Lucy resigns herself to sorrow/In building character for tomorrow./Lucy tells us to carry on,/It's always darkest before the dawn.* In his last lines, he exhorted us: *Let's go over to Lucy's house/And let's lynch Lucy!*

I share Nash's exasperation with the sort of people who manage to tell you, when you're steeped in emotional pain, when the world is upside down for you, when you are overwhelmed by circumstances—be positive! Don't worry! Put on a happy face! I share Nash's exasperation, but I doubt it would be useful—Lucy would probably find some way to put a positive spin on it.

In my last article I mentioned a woman I have never met but admire. She is a bright light in the midst of worldly and personal darkness. She encourages people to look for good in others, to believe in goodness, and some of that goodness she calls God. Lately, I have come to admire her even more because I have learnt, by way of postings she has made, that she is wrestling with depression and anxiety.

Shortly after I wrote that article, I was given a hefty amount of 'advice' which could easily have come from Lucy Lake. 'Be positive, be happy, greet the day with a smile!' One person posted something to convey her frustrations (presumably with me) because she's sad and sorry that people go through difficulties and she can't help them, no matter how hard she tries. Her audience chimed in with such remarks as 'they can't be helped because they don't want to be helped,' and 'they choose to be the way they are.'

This coincided with a tragedy in the life of a friend—her husband died, and she is understandably distraught and miserable. Shall we assume that my friend is choosing to be sad? A few years ago the home of eleven people burnt to the ground and our worlds were turned upside down. Our perspectives, our attitudes, even our personalities were irreparably altered by this event. The direction of our hopes for our lives was irrevocably changed by external events. Some of us have endured lasting injury. How was this our choice?

There is absolutely nothing wrong with a balanced, optimistic viewpoint. It is undoubtedly more uplifting to see good things, to be happy, and to view events as opportunities for improvement. If you believe in God, by all means put your faith, trust, and hope in Him. If you do not, you have other things in which you can put your faith, if nothing more than statistical probability. A coin, tossed in the air enough times, will eventually come up 'heads' 50% of the time, and the prolonged run of bad luck or misfortune you've had will eventually run out. Many of those terrible things you experienced may actually turn out to be foundation stones for something positive. There is nothing wrong with patiently waiting for positive change, but that wait may be incredibly painful. You know it, and other people need to respect it.

Those changes and improvements will happen in their own time. Exhorting someone to 'snap out of it', 'pull yourself together', or a cheery but thin 'it will be all right' does not help. In fact, it may cause even more hurt.

When I've been subjected to this positivistic counselling, I've always felt judged for not being in the same place mentally or emotionally that other people are. The young woman I mentioned is a devout Christian, yet others of her faith criticize her for 'choosing' to remain anxious and depressed (despite her depression and anxiety having a physical basis which she cannot control).

No one can possibly feel so bad that they cannot be made to feel worse, as is proven again and again.

It's a question of balance—how much optimism can a person afford, given the current conditions or events? It's also a question of timing. Who is insensitive enough to go to a new widow and say, 'Now you can date again,' or to someone with depression and anxiety disorders and say 'your faith is not strong enough. You don't BELIEVE!' There is no benefit in blaming the victim.

If it were a simple matter of 'pulling yourself together' or 'snapping out of it,' don't you think that would have been done already?

Here's my plan. When we leave Lucy Lake's house, let's go over to the house of that guy who came up with 'don't worry, be happy!' and have a serious talk with him.

If you are dealing with PTSD, Chronic Depression, Anxiety Disorders, or other forms of psychological 'illness', please be assured you are *not* at fault, and *you are not alone.*

☩☩☩

Faith 2015
31 December 2015

Last year at this time, I wrote a piece, 'The Class of 2014', in which I gave a summary of my year, and pointed out the good things that had happened. I was quite happy to see how many people read it, and better, revisited it, throughout the year. I thought I'd do the same this year, although the 'spin' has to be different.

During the last twelve months, I've lost my home (again), relocated to an area of the country to stay with people with whom, ultimately, I did not feel safe. After considerable turmoil, I returned to the middle West very hastily, and at great expense. Now I'm camping on someone's couch, at their tremendous inconvenience, with the hope of avoiding the trauma of a homeless shelter in my immediate future. I interacted a spectrum of people ranging from with people who insisted on treating me like a child (which is humiliating), to people who expected too much—they don't understand conditions like PTSD or Anxiety Disorders, and the limitations such conditions impose (which is frustrating). Curiously, those who did the one often did the second as well.

It has not been a stellar year.

Although there was a lot of negativity in 2015, there were positives as well. I discovered, for example, that I meant something to a young lady of ten, even though I had to leave before she could express that feeling. I discovered the selflessness of friendship, going above and beyond anyone's reasonable expectations. I learnt something about being forgiven and embraced after many years' absence. I found 'keep it simple' to be a very useful rule of thumb, and learnt not to worry, or to plan, beyond the next meal. I learnt to accept that in every situation, there is a certain element of the unknown that must be taken into account in any expectation because Surprise is part of the Universal Experience. Predictability is a bore and life is anything but boring....

I was also reminded of a very old lesson—actions speak louder than words. What makes a person a good Christian is not whether they've read the Bible from cover to cover, but what they've done with what they've read. The wisest people are not those with the catchiest clichés, but the most profound silences. I've also learnt that some of the best people are those who suffer the most. They know what it is to listen because they have known what it was not to be heard.

I learnt a lot about faith and here I have to make some distinctions. I don't mean the Pollyanna-type faith expressed in mindless optimism, or the saccharin faith that (big sappy grin) 'The Lord will provide' because it said so in a Sunday school song. No clouds part to let a brilliant sun shine through, nor do choruses of angels intone 'Ahhhhhh' in heavenly wise.

I mean the faith that comes from living in hard times and surviving. Consequently, when my friend said 'It will work out,' I knew she was speaking from experience, and to my joy, she was not wrong (though the fruits of faith sometimes blossom s-l-o-w-l-y).

Although it was difficult, in time I found myself thinking her way.

We've discussed faith before. It is a vital element of being human, it is easiest to have when things go well, and most important (as well as most difficult) to have when having faith is most needed. There are very few people in the world who have had an easy time with life. Pain is relative—the disappointment that annoys me might devastate you, and yet, you might find it easier than I to believe that no matter how long it takes, 'joy cometh in the morning.' We all have endured disheartenment and sorrow, and we all have survived it. These are the lessons 2015 gave to me.

Why is Faith vital?

What do you have without it?

༺✦༻

Paul TN Chapman
ptnc.books@gmail.com

Made in the USA
Columbia, SC
08 May 2025